AF564700

WILD LIFE LAWS AND ITS IMPACT ON TRIBES

WILD LIFE LAWS AND ITS IMPACT ON TRIBES

MONA PUROHIT
Ph.D. (Law), LL.M. (Modern Legal Studies)
Sr. Lecturer, Deptt. of Law,
Rani Durgavati Vishwavidyalaya, Jabalpur

DEEP & DEEP PUBLICATIONS PVT. LTD.
F-159, Rajouri Garden, New Delhi - 110 027

WILD LIFE LAWS AND ITS IMPACT ON TRIBES

ISBN 978-81-8450-014-1

Typeset by RAHUL COMPOSERS
358, Sector 16-B, Phase-II, Pocket-B, Dwarka, New Delhi - 110 075

Printed in India at MAYUR ENTERPRISES
WZ Plot No. 3, Gujjar Market, Tihar Village, New Delhi - 110 018

Published by DEEP & DEEP PUBLICATIONS PVT. LTD.
F-159, Rajouri Garden, New Delhi - 110 027
Phone : 25435369, 25440916
E-mail : deep98@del3.vsnl.net.in • ddpbooks@yahoo.co.in
Showroom :
2/13, Ansari Road, Daryaganj, New Delhi - 110 002 • Telefax : 23245122

In the memory of

my father

R.D. PUROHIT

Contents

Acknowledgements

At the very outset I owe my gratitude for the completion of this book to none else but 'Sainath' the 'Almighty',—who I believe, is the spiritual force behind all creation. Next comes the inspiration, which came to me in the form of my guide Dr. Divya Chansoria, whose confidence in me provided me with the desired strength and vigour required to accomplish such a stupendous task. My wavering mind and rambling thoughts could be directed to this modest critical effort only at her stance and for such indulgence in me I can only pray to God for the fulfillment of her ideals.

To Dr. Alok Chansoria, I owe special gratitude, who despite his extremely busy schedule and hectic public life spared valuable time for the work. His critical insight helped me remove all obscurities that cropped-up in my mind during the study.

I owe the perseverance required co accomplish such a work to my husband, Mr. K.K. Shukla, whose assistance persuasion and moral support resulted in this fruitful endeavour. It was he who severally directed my rambling thoughts. I must admit, it was impossible for me to reach my destination without his support.

Aman, my son's contribution to this work is irreplacable and deserve special gratitude, as the book stands on the foundation of his precious time which I have encroached upon.

My mother Mrs. Asha Purohit's blessings and encouragement was boundless and cannot be expressed in words. My gratitude knows no bounds to my affectionate mother-in-law Mrs. Susheela Shukla, father-in-law Mr. H.R. Shukla, Brother-in-laws, Kailash and Vinod, Sister-in-law Mrs. Rekha

Tiwari, who gave me strong moral support during some critical moments of failure and frustration from the beginning to the end of this book.

Mr. Prasoon, Praveen, Prabhey and Pranaya, my brothers made it sure that I should not loose hope in this long journey. How can I forget them and their wives Vatsala, Krishna, Aparna and Shilpa's admonition and words of promotion.

I owe my gratitude to Deep & Deep Publications Pvt. Ltd., New Delhi, for its readiness to publish my work.

Jabalpur MONA PUROHIT

Introduction

Wild Life (Protection) Act, 1972 covers 521 National Parks and Sanctuaries in India, which covers 4.5 percent of the territorial areas. This vast network of Protected Areas (PA), as it is called, has helped in the conservation of a significant part of Indian biodiversity, which includes a wide range of natural habitats, plants and animal species. At the same time, this conservation process has given birth to serious conflicts between the tribal communities dependent on the natural resources of these areas and the protected areas managers.

According to all modern theories, any protection policy without collaboration with the local people is unjust to them and is an infringement of their fundamental rights, as also unprofitable for the conservation of wild life. Such a policy is bound to raise conflicts, which become a serious threat for the policy itself.

The tribal communities have traditionally been a great support in the conservation of natural habitats in forest areas. Its knowledge about local biodiversity is subtle and useful. What is required is the evolution of a process through which the local communities and wild life conservation could work together with peace and harmony.

The problem of biodiversity conservation has rightly drawn the attention of world community. Many international organisations have come forward with their very important resolutions and suggestions in this area. The conflict between the local communities and the institution of biodiversity conservation is not limited to India alone. It has its occurrence in many other countries which have tribal people known as the indigenous people.

Notable amongst them are the Hupa Indians of Northern California, the Inuit of Isabella, Bay in Canada, the Zoque Indians of Mexico, the Karen of Thailand, the Shona people in Zimbabwe, the Kuna of Panama, the Simshali of Pakistan, the Phoka people of Northern Malawi, the Imagruen of Mauritania, the Ewenk of Siberia, and many others scattered all over the globe.[1]

The book stresses upon the study of some important international and national laws related to the protection of wild life and the tribal laws.

Objective

There are strong laws and provisions for the preservation of wild life and the protection of rights of the Scheduled Tribes in India. As the area of inhabitation of the tribesmen is very closely related and even overlap with the Reserved Forest Areas, there is bound to occur instances of conflicts and disturbances between them. Under the Constitution of India there are a number of provisions for the welfare of both, yet due to inadequate provisions and at times wrongful interpretation or implementation and also due to ignorance of law, there has been innumerable instances of disagreements and contradictions.

Government of India is duty bound to protect the rights of the tribal people. Despite 55 years of freedom there living conditions remain unimproved. Education and literacy still remain a matter of dream for them. It is due to lack of education that they are absolutely ignorant of laws moreso the forest laws. On the other hand, it is also incumbent upon the Government of India to preserve wild life. Thoughtless deforestation in the present time has further endangered the animal life. Besides, it has furthered the problem of ecological imbalance. Environmental pollution is another problem, which poses a potent threat to the preservation of wild life. Keeping all these factors in mind the Government of India has made a number of laws and enforced various rules and policies.

As the wild life has been accorded statutory protection, it seems to me that the tribesmen have been deprived of their fundamental rights of livelihood.

The so-called. advocates of wild life conservation have entirely ignored the basic needs of the tribal people awarded to them by nature, justly and properly. It is this aspect, which has to be elaborately taken up in this book. At the same time it should also be proposed that the restrictions which are to be imposed on tribesmen to protect wild life should side by side provide adequate relief to the tribal people, so that their natural ways of living may not be disturbed.

Ashish Kothari observes the situation thus:

> Those who are advocating the cause of tribals and other local traditional communities are speaking the language of universal human rights. Quite justifiably, they argue that rights to land, dwelling, livelihood and cultural identity are inalienable and that any attempt to take away these rights in the name of development or conservation is unacceptable. They also point out that in most cases these people are the original human inhabitants of the area and therefore should have a decisive say in how the area's resources are managed and utilised.[2]

It should also be kept in mind that while providing concessions to the tribal people they should also be educated not to create pollution, which adversely affects the wild life.

The book is concerned with the problems arising out of the implementation of laws pertaining to the protection of wild life and its impact upon the rights of the tribal people. The purpose of this book is to make a critical analysis of the existing laws related to the welfare of the tribal people and the preservation of wild life and also to suggest legal remedies and measures so as to remove disharmony and discord between them.

The tribal life of India has a long history. The Britishers adopted two policies for them. One was for the removal of certain evil customs, which were prevalent in the society, like *sati*, child marriage, etc., and the other was the policy of non-interference in the recognition of their customary laws about marriage, adoption, succession, etc.

Even after the independence of India, the situation has not changed much. As the Constitution guarantees "equal rights for all" the tribal people are no exception to it. In addition to this the

Constitution also provides some special welfare provisions for them.

There are many laws for the Scheduled Tribes and at the same time they have their own customary or traditional code of conduct too. The legislative provisions are of two types. One for their welfare and the other that puts restrictions on their conduct.

There are many laws to protect the environment. Some of them are; Wild Life (Protection) Act, 1972, Indian Forest Act, 1927, etc. These Acts protect the wild life by declaring some areas as Protected Areas, Reserved Forests, Protected Forests, etc. These Acts also affect the tribal laws, which are made for the welfare of the tribesmen.

Notes and References

1. A WWF International Position Paper, Dr. Claude Martin, Director General, Dr. Chris Hails, Programme Director, Gland, Switzerland, 22 May 1996.
2. Ashish Kothari: "Is Joint Management of Protected Areas, Desirable and Possible?" Editors: Ashish Kothari, Neena Singh, Saloni Suri "People and Protected Areas" Towards Participatory Conservation in India, Sage Publications, New Delhi, p. 19.

1

International Measures and Laws of some Countries to Protect the Wild Life

The danger to ecology has become a very serious problem at which urgent attention is now being paid in most part of the world. In order to maintain the ecological balance wild life protection is also one important aspect. Internationally, many efforts have been made in this area. The object of this chapter is to discuss the International measures and the laws which have been enforced from time to time in different countries to protect the wild life.

Socio-legal Aspects

Wild life conservation has scientific, legal and economic components. For the successful conservation of it all these aspects should be taken into consideration. The lawmaker must understand human action and socio-cultural traditions.

Forest and Wild Life

The issue of protection of wild life is tagged with the protection of forests. Since the habitat of wild, animals is forest, wild animals and forest are inseparable from each other. All over the world the devastation of wild life is on a higher scale than the devastation of forests. Both are so interlinked that no international or national policy or law can conserve the wild life without preserving the forests.

Global Concern—Wild Life

In the ancient times the need to protect wild life was perceived solely in human terms which resulted in the protection of the animals and plants in a natural state but very few laws were made specifically for the protection of wild life. The disturbance in the ecological balance later attracted the attention of the international community towards the protection of environment which includes wild life.

Different countries for the protection of wild life have formulated different laws. With respect to the limitations of this research work it will not be proper to discuss all of them in detail. At the same time declarations, conferences, treaties and conventions, particularly those in which India has been one of the participants, have been taken into consideration.

Declaration on the Permanent Sovereignty over Natural Resources, 1962

General Assembly Resolution of 1962 on Permanent Sovereignty over Natural Resources Resolution 1803 (XVII)

The General Assembly

Recalling its resolution 523 (VI) of 12 January 1952 and 626(vii) of 21 December, 1952. Bearing in mind resolution 1314 (XIII) of 12 December, 1958, by which it established the Commission on Permanent Sovereignty over Natural Resources and instructed it to conduct a full survey of the status of permanent sovereignty over natural wealth and resources as a basic constituent of the right to self-determination, with recommendations, where necessary, for its strengthening, and decided further that, in the conduct of the full survey of the status of the permanent sovereignty of people and nations over their natural wealth and resources, due regard should be paid to the rights and duties of States under international law and to the importance of encouraging international co-operation in the economic development of developing countries.

Many declarations were given, under the said resolution. One of which throws light on the natural rights of the people is stated below:

> Foreign investment agreements freely entered into by, or between, sovereign States shall be observed in good faith; States and international organizations shall strictly and conscientiously respect—the sovereignty of peoples and nations over their natural wealth and resources in accordance with the Charter and the principles set forth III the present resolution.[1]

From this we can infer that the international community respects the rights of the people over their natural wealth and resources. An important role in this direction is being played by the World Conservation Union which organises the Congress every ten years "to take stock of Protected Areas (PAs), appraise progress and setbacks, and chart the course for PAs over the next decade."[2]

First World Conference on National Parks (Seattle, US) 30th June—7 July 1962),

> aimed to establish a more effective international understanding of national parks and to encourage further development of the national park movement worldwide. Issues discussed included: the effects of human on wild life; species extinction; the religious significance and aesthetic meaning of certain parks and wilderness; international supervision of boundary parks; the economic benefits of tourist; the role of national parks in scientific studies; and some practical problems related to park management.[3]

Meeting of International Union for the Conservation of Nature and Natural Resources, 1969

This meeting was held in India and the Conservationists, who were present were intimately familiar with Indian forest and wild life. They sounded the alarms about the disappearance of tigers. Trade in tiger parts, especially skins, largely came under control with the advent of the International convention in 1975.

The Second World Conference on National Parks

(Yellow stone, US, 18-27 September, 1972),

addressed: the effects of tourism on protected areas; broad aspects of park planning and management; special social, scientific and environmental problems within national parks in wet tropical, arid and mountain regions, controversial aspects of wild life management in PAs; the social scientific and environmental problems of marine, island, polar and sub-polar PAs, the problem associated with communicating park values to visitors and raising environmental awareness; international training opportunities; opportunities to expand and improve the global park system; and the need for and benefits of public support for PAs.[4]

Stockholm Conference of 1972 on the Human Environment

The United Nations is concerned about the world-wide problems of maintaining safe environment for the human beings. In total 119 countries participated in this conference few of them were U.S.A., Malaysia, China, Kenya, Soviet Union, including India which also was an active participant. A declaration was made with the main objective to solve the global problems of conservation and regulation of human environment by international agreement on a universal level. "Having considered the need for a common outlook and for common principle inspire and guide the peoples of the world in the preservation and enhancement human environment."[5]

Many principles were laid down in this declaration. Some of them are directly concerned with the protection of wild life.

They are as follows:

Principle 2 states: The natural resources of the earth including the air, water, land, flora and fauna especially representative samples of natural ecosystems must be safeguarded for the benefit of present and future generations through careful planning or management, as appropriate.[6] *Principle 4 states*: Man has a special responsibility to safeguard and wisely manage the heritage of wild life and its habitat, which are now gravely imperilled by a combination of adverse factors. Nature conservation including wild life must therefore receive importance in planning for economic development. [7]

Convention for the Protection of the World Cultural and Natural Heritage, 1972

The General Conference of the United Nations Education, Scientific and Cultural Organization meeting in Paris from 17 October to 21 November, 1972 met for the convention. In November 1992 the convention had been ratified by 129 nations in which India was also a party.

As per Article 2: *"For the purpose of this Convention, the following shall be considered as "natural heritage":*

natural features consisting of physical and biological formations or groups of such formations, which are of outstanding universal value from the aesthetic or scientific point of view. Geological and physiographical formations and precisely delineated areas, which constitute the habitat of threatened species of animals and plants of outstanding universal value from the point of view of science or conservation.[8]

Many objectives were outlined in the following convention but a reference has been made below to only those, which deal with "natural heritage".

Noting that the cultural heritage and the natural heritage are increasingly threatened with destruction not only by the traditional causes of decay, but also by changing social and economic conditions which aggravate the situation with even more formidable phenomena of damage or destruction, Considering that parts of the cultural or natural heritage are of outstanding inter and therefore need to be preserved as part of the world heritage of mankind as a whole.[9]

Article 6(1) in part-II of the Convention i.e., National Protection and International Protection of the Cultural and Natural Heritage says:

> Whilst fully respecting the sovereignty of the States on whose territory the cultural and natural heritage mentioned in Articles 1 and 2 is situated, and without protection to property right provided by national legislation, the States Parties to this Convention recognize that such heritage constitutes a world heritage for whose protection is the duty of the international community as a whole to co-operate.[10]

Convention on International Trade in Endangered Species of Wild Fauna and Flora, 1973: (As amended in 1979)

Entry into force; 1 July 1975,

This is an important convention stressing on the conservation of the Endangered species of Wild fauna and flora. Certain relevant recognitions which are made by the contracting states are as follows:

> RECOGNIZING that wild fauna and flora in their many beautiful and varied forms are an irreplaceable part of the natural systems of the earth which must be protected for this and the generations to come; CONSCIOUS of the ever-growing value of wild fauna and flora from aesthetic, scientific, cultural, recreational and economic points of view; RECOGNIZING that people and State are and should be the best protectors of their own wild fauna and flora; RECOGNIZING, in addition, that international cooperation is essential for the protection of certain species of wild fauna and flora against over exploitation through international trade.[11]

A reference to the measures to be taken by the parties to enforce the provisions of this convention and to prohibit trade in specimens is made: "(a) to penalize trade in, or possession of, such specimens, or both; and (b) to provide for the confiscation or return to the State of export of such specimens."[12] "Specimen" as per this convention will be "an animal or plant, whether alive or deed."[13] This shows that wild life in not excluded.

The World Charter for Nature, 1982

The United Nation General Assembly, on Oct. 28, 1982 adopted, "World Charter for Nature", which reasserted "that man is a part of nature, life depends on natural systems, which ensure supply of energy and nutrients, provide opportunities for development of his creativity and also for rest and recreation."[14]

World Charter for nature laid down certain general principles of conservation by which all human conduct affecting nature is to be guided and judged. They are as follows:

1. Nature shall be respected and its essential processes shall not be impaired.
2. The genetic viability on the earth shall not be compromised; the population level of all life forms, wild and domesticated, must be at least sufficient for their survival, and to this end necessary habitats shall be safeguarded.
3. All areas of the earth, both land and sea, shall be subject to these principles of conservation; special protection shall be given to unique areas, to representative samples of all the different types of ecosystems and to the habitats of rare or endangered species.
4. Ecosystems and organisms, as well as the land, marine and atmospheric resources that are utilized by man, shall be managed to achieve and maintain optimum sustainable productivity, but not in such a way as to endanger the integrity of those other ecosystems or species with which they coexist.[15]

Earth Summit or United Nations Conference on Environment and Development (UNCED) 1992

This conference was organised from 3rd June to 14th June 1992 in Rio-de-Janario, the capital of Brazil. 178 Nations participated in it and India was also present as one of the signatories. In this summit it was decided that deep introspection regarding the rapid degradation of sea birds and fisheries living in polluted water is required. The main achievements of the Earth Summit were:

(i) Rio Declaration
(ii) Agenda 21
(iii) Convention on Bio-diversity
(iv) Convention on Climate change
(v) Convention on Forestry.

Rio Declaration and Agenda 21 were accepted by all the States and Convention on Climate change, Convention on Biodiversity and Convention on Forestry were signed by 150 countries. India was also one of them.

In this declaration, agenda 21, which contains a set of principles for the conduct of peoples and nations towards each other and the Earth, was adopted. This is document of 900 pages and contains some very important issues like the skilful use of forest and bio-diversity, protection of sea, etc. Dr. S.K. Kapoor in his book International Law and Human Rights writes:

> The convention on Forests also generated a lot of controversy from the very beginning. While the rich nations wanted to control massive deforestation through a convention, the developing countries regarded it as infringement on their sovereignty. Developing countries including India had serious reservations on forest principles contained in the draft. These countries led by India succeeded in getting the said provisions changed. Thus consensus was reached on provisions relating to sustained development of forests.[16]

The principles laid down under the Earth Summit (1992) were regarded as persuasive and weak. The developing countries felt the need for assessment for their adequacy as forests are essential for—the economic development of any developing nation.

In the Convention on Biological Diversity, 1992 which is one of the achievements of the Earth Summit the contracting parties affirmed that the conservation of biological diversity is a common concern of human kind and that the States are responsible for conserving their biological diversity and for using their biological resources in a sustainable manner. It showed its concern over the significant reduction of biological diversity by certain human activities.

Certain objectives given under the CBD in which India became a Party in 1994 were:

1. Protection of the gene of fauna and flora.
2. For the protection of the Fauna and Flora. State should adopt some legal measures.
3. It also acknowledges a value of conservation practices and knowledge of Tribal, herders, fishers, and peasants effective and practical way to preserve biological diversity.

In the year 1992 The World Conservation Union organised the fourth World Congress on National Parks and Protected Areas: Parks for Life (Caracas, Venezuela, 10-21 February, 1992) which emphasized:

> the relationship between people and PAs, and the need for: the identification of sites of importance of biodiversity conservation; a regional approach to land management; investments as part of an overall development package; and building a stronger constituency for conservation. The Caracas Action Plan synthesized the strategic actions for PAs over the decade 1992-2002 and provided a global framework for collective action four objectives: integrating PAs into wider planning frameworks; expanding the support for PAs by involving local communities and other non-traditional interest groups; strengthening the capacity to manage PAs; and expanding international co-operation for the financing, development and management of PAs. The Plan aimed to extend the PA network to cover at least 10% of each major biome by the year 2000.

First Ministerial Conference of the Forestry Forum for Developing Countries (FFDC), 1993

It was held from 1st to 3rd September, 1993 in Delhi in which representatives of developed countries, 40 developing countries and observers of different international institutions have participated. Forest principles of Rio Declaration are needed to be adopted and prohibition of the cutting of trees, forest rehabilitation and afforestation.

World Congress on National Parks, 1982

This congress meeting was held in Bali, Indonesia focusing specifically on current options for the maintenance of biological diversity and examined 120 prepared case studies from various regions. A total of more than 500 scientists and other specialists examined the status of protected areas and the link between biological conservation and sustainable development.

Brazil—US International Experts Meeting on Protected Forest Areas (1999)

The government of Brazil and the United States of America sponsored the meeting from 15 to 19 March, 1999. The "goal of the international experts meeting was to distil the wisdom of expert world wide into succinct conclusions and practical recommendations." In addition to Brazil and United States, Contact group members included Australia, Chili, France, India, Japan, Malaysia United Kingdom, Zimbabwe and the IUCN and World Bank.

Based on the discussions, the contact group identified the following five key topics as the organizing themes of the meeting which are outlined below:

(a) Classification systems for protected forest areas;
(b) Management effectiveness for protected forest areas;
(c) Criteria for establishing protected forest areas;
(d) Economic viability of protected forest areas;
(e) The benefit's and mechanisms for protecting forest areas.[17]

Parks Congress: Reconciling Protected Areas and Sustainable Livelihoods (2003)

From 8 to 17 September, IUCN—The World Conservation Union convened the fifth World Parks Congress (WPC) meeting which was held in Durban, South Africa. The theme was "Benefits Beyond Boundaries" which dealt with the issue "how to ensure that the benefits of protected areas are conserved and shared in an equal manner."[18] It was for the first time that high and active participation of a diverse range of indigenous groups was visualized. The Durban Accord provides certain benefits for the indigenous peoples and also highlights that:

> a rapidly changing world has resulted in an increasing loss of biological and cultural diversity and stresses the important role protected areas play in halting this loss as well as in achieving border development goals. Furthermore the Accord stresses the importance of the wisdom and knowledge held by various cultures enabling the sustainable use and conservation of biodiversity, and acknowledges that protected areas are important providers of ecosystem goods and services. Reflecting the overall theme of benefits beyond boundaries and the large participation of indigenous groups and peoples in the WPC, participants stressed that while many costs of protected areas are borne locally particularly by poor communities—benefits accrue globally and remain under-appreciated and are not shared with local communities.[19]

The major outcome of this accord can be cited in the words of South African Environmental Affairs Minister Valli Moosa:

> We have established a link very firmly between ecosystems and communities. It's a new paradigm and there is no going back from here. He furthermore highlighted that the Congress had identified how protected areas could be used as a tool in poverty alleviation efforts. Kenton Millor, Chair of the IUCNs World Commission on Protected Areas also emphasised that "Today's agenda recognises the benefits [of Protected Areas] and ensures that they are equitably shared. In 2013 we will be able to look back and hopeful be proud of our new achievements."[20]

Some more Conventions other than those Discussed above are Laid Down below for Perusal

1. Convention for protection of animal and vegetable of the State. (1936)
2. The International Convention for the Regulation of Whaling. (1946)

3. Convention on wetland of International importance especially as Waterfowl Habitat. (1971)
4. Convention for Protection of World Culture and National Habitat. (1972)
5. The Conservation of European Wild life and Natural Habitats. (1979)
6. The Bona Convention on the Conservation of Migratory Species of Wilds Animals. (1979)

To implement these Conventions in a better manner the organisation like IUCN, WWF, UNDP, UNEP etc. were established. Lot of work has been done for the conservation of biological resources by these organisations.

After a brief discussion of the various international measures adopted to protect the wild life in the first part of Chapter 1, I feel the necessity to study Wild Life laws of various countries like Japan, Canada, China, Malawi and Bulgaria in the second part before coming of Indian laws for the protection of wild life in Chapter 2. Before coming to the Acts of the different countries I would like to acknowledge mention the source of this information, i.e. internet. There is nothing original in this except the categorisation and segregation of the various lanes but the originality lies in the comparisons made and the observations drawn at the end of Chapter 2. Name of the Wild Life Acts of the different countries taken for study are as follows: *Protected Areas Law (1998) Bulgaria, Canada Wild Life Act (1985), Law of the People's Republic of China on the Protection of Wild life, Wild Life Protection and Hunting Law and Related Legislation (1918), Japan, Malawi National Parks and Wild life Act (1992).* Only those provisions, which were relevant to this work, have been taken into consideration. These are enlisted below:

(1) Authority.
(2) Ownership of the Wild Life.
(3) Categories of Protected Areas.
(4) Declaration of Protected Areas for Wild Life.
(5) Procedure for Acquisition of Lands.
(6) Administrative Provisions.
(7) Penal Provisions.
(8) Settlement of the Rights of the Tribes.

AUTHORITY

Bulgaria

Article 48

Regional authorities of the Ministry of Environment and Waters concerned with protected areas shall be the Park Directorates and the Regional Inspectorates of Environment and Waters.[1]

Canada

Section 11

(1) The Minister may designate any person or class of persons to act as wild life officers for the purposes of this Act and the regulations.

Designation of Provincial Government Employees

(2) The Minister may not designate any person or class of persons employed by the government of a province unless that government agrees.

Certificate of Designation

(3) Every wild life officer must be provided with a certificate of designation as a wild life officer in a form approved by the Minister and, on entering any place under this Act, the officer shall, if so requested, show the certificate to the occupant or person in charge of the place.

Power of Peace Officers

(4) For the purposes of this Act and the regulations, wild life officers have all the powers of a peace officer, but the

1. http://www. international wildlife law.org/legislat.shtmll Bulgaria.htm

Minister may specify limits on those powers when designating any person or class of persons.[2]

China

Article 7

The departments of forestry and fishery administration under the State Council shall be respectively responsible for the nationwide administration of terrestrial and aquatic wild life.

The departments of forestry administration under the governments of provinces, autonomous regions and municipalities directly under the Central Government shall be responsible for the administration of terrestrial wild life in their respective areas. The departments in charge of the administration of terrestrial wild life in their respective areas. The departments in charge of the administration of terrestrial wild life under the governments of autonomous prefectures, counties and municipalities shall be designated by the governments of provinces, autonomous regions or municipalities directly under the Central Government.

The departments of fishery administration under the local governments at or above the country level shall be responsible for the administration of aquatic wild life in their respective areas.[3]

Japan

Article 1-2

The prefectural governor, in order to execute the project aiming at the protection and propagation of game (inclusive of the control with respect to hunting thereof. Hereinafter referred to as game protection project) in accordance with the standard specified by the Director-General of the Environment Agency upon hearing the opinion of the Nature Conservation Council, shall set up the game protection project plan.[4]

2. http://www. international wildlifelaw.org/legislat.shtml/Canada.ht
3. http://www.international wildlife law. org/legislat.shtml/china.htm
4. http://www.international wildlifelaw.org/legislat.shtml/japan.htm

Malawi

Section 2 of Part I

"Officer" means the Chief Parks and Wild life Officer and any other officer appointed pursuant to section 5.

Section 5 of Part II

For the purpose of implementing this Act, there shall be appointed in the public service an officer to the designated as the Chief Parks and Wild life Officer and other officers subordinate to him who shall be responsible for the administration of this Act subject to any general of special directions of the Minister.

Section 7 of Part II

(1) The Minister may appoint any person to be an Honorary Parks and Wild life Officer for such period not exceeding three years as the Minister shall specify in the instrument of appointment, renewal or revocation to be published in the Gazette.

(2) The appointment of any Honorary Parks and Wild life Officer may be—

(a) general, in which case it shall authorize the officer to act in any part of Malawi, or

(b) limited, authorizing the officer to act only within a specified part or specified parts of Malawi.

(3) An Honorary Parks and Wild life Officer may at any time be called by the Chief Parks and Wild life Officer to serve on such official duties under this Act and for such length of time as may be agreed between the officer and the Chief Parks and Wild life Officer.

(4) Every Honorary Parks and Wild life Officer appointed under this section shall, while on official duty, be subject to the directions of the Chief Parks and Wild life Officer or other officers appointed under this Act.[5]

5. http://www. international wildlife law.org/legislat.shtml/malavi.htm

OWNERSHIP OF THE WILD LIFE

Here Ownership means the acquisition requisition and possession of the wild life and their habitat.

Bulgaria

Article 8

(1) The parks of national significance stated in Annex. 1 and the nature reserves stated in Annex. 2 of the Act, which are used for the serving for the satisfaction of public needs of nation-wide significance shall be exclusively the exclusive property of the State owned by of the state and are indicated in an Annex hereto.

(2) The Parks of national significance shall be areas under Article 5, item 2, that include natural ecosystems of large diversity of plant and animal species and habitats, and are larger than 3 0000 1000 ha. and do not include any populated areas. Their boundaries shall not include populated areas and settlement formations, monasteries, lands and forests around these, the ownership of which shall be restored under the Agricultural Land Ownership and Use Act and the Forest and Forest Fund Ownership Restoration Act.

(3) the nature reserves shall be areas under Article 5, item 1 and item 4 that include models of natural ecosystems whose conservation shall exclude any, or allow for minimum, human intervention.

Canada

"Public Lands" "Terres Domaniales"

"Public lands" means lands belonging to Her Majesty in right of Canada and lands that the Government of Canada has power to dispose of, subject to the terms of any agreement between the Government of Canada and the government of the province in which the lands are situated, and includes :

(a) any waters on or flowing through the lands and the natural resources of the lands, and
(b) the internal waters and the territorial sea of Canada.

China

Article 3

Wild life resources shall be owned by the State (I)- Set 39 Wild animals to be Govt. Property.

The State shall protect the lawful rights and interests of units and individuals engaged in the development or utilization of wildlife resources according to law.

Japan

After a detailed study of the wild life protection and hunting law and related legislation (1918). I have not come across any such provision, which states the ownership of the wild life.

Malawi

Section 4 of Part 1

The ownership of every wild animal and wild plant existing in its wild habitat in Malawi is vested in the President on behalf of, and for the benefit of the people of Malawi.

CATEGORIES OF PROTECTED AREAS

Bulgaria

Article 5

The protected area categories shall be:

1. Strict Nature Reserve;
2. National park;
3. Natural monument;
4. Managed reserve;
5. Natural park;
6. Protected site.

Canada

After a detailed study of the Canada Wildlife Act (1985). I have not come across any such provision, which states the categories of protected areas.

China

Article 20

In nature reserves and areas closed to hunting, and during seasons closed to hunting, the hunting and catching of wildlife and other activities which are harmful to the living and breeding of wildlife shall be prohibited.

The areas and seasons closed to hunting as well as the prohibited hunting gear and methods shall be specified by governments at or above the county level or by the departments of wildlife administration under them.

Japan

In Japan the 3 categories have been seen (a) sanctuary, (b) designation of special sanctuary, (c) establishment of temporary hunting prohibited area.

Malawi

"protected area" includes national park, wildlife reserve and forest reserve.

In Malawi there are three categories of protected areas: National Park, Wild Life Reserve and Forest Reserve.

PROCEDURE OF DECLARATION OF PROTECTED AREAS FOR WILD LIFE

Bulgaria

The declaration and changes within the protected areas shall be made by the Minister of Environment and Waters.

Article 11

1. The owners and users of forests, lands and aquatic areas within protected areas shall observe the regiments

established hereunder by means of with the protected area declaration order and with the management plan.

Article 12

1. Real estates within the protected areas shall be disposed of following presentation of a written declaration by the transfer or as to whether the property is within a protected area.

Article 16

1. Declared as reserves shall be model natural ecosystems that include typical and/or remarkable wild plant and animal species and their habitats.

Canada

After a detailed study of the Canada Wildlife Act (1985). I have not come across any such provision, which states the procedure for declaration of protect areas of wild life.

China

Article 6

The governments at various levels shall strengthen the administration of wildlife resources and formulate plans and measures for the protection, development and rational utilization of wildlife resources.

Japan

Article 8-2

The Director-General of the Environment Agency or the Prefectural Governor, when he deems it necessary for protection and propagation of game, may, in accordance with the provision of the Cabinet Order, establish the sanctuary.

The person who has a right of ownership or other rights with respect to the land or standing trees or bamboos inside of the boundary of the sanctuary shall not reject the establishment of facilities of nesting, water supply and feeding needed for breeding and propagation of game on the land or standing trees or bamboos concerned by the Director-General of the Environment Agency or the Prefectural Governor.

The Director-General of the Environment Agency or the Prefectural Governor when he deems it necessary for protection and propagation of game, shall, in accordance with the provision of the Cabinet Order specify the special sanctuary inside of the boundary of the sanctuary.

The provisions of paragraphs 4 and 5 of Article 1-4 shall apply mutates to the case of paragraph 1 and the preceding paragraph.

The person who intends to make filling up of the water surface, or reclamation, felling of standing trees and bamboos or establishment of any structure shall be required for permission of the Director-General of the Environment Agency or the prefectural governor except the action which shall be deemed no hindrance to the protection and propagation of which shall be deemed no hindrance to the protection and propagation of game and specified by the Director-General of the Environment Agency or the construction of minor structure which is specified by the prefectural governor.

In case where the application for permission of the preceding paragraph is made, the Director-General of the Environment Agency or the Prefectural Governor shall not reject the application unless the action with respect to the application involves the justifiable reason in which there is a hindrance to the protection and propagation of game in the special sanctuary concerned.

The State or prefecture shall compensate the loss to be occurred naturally to the person who suffered a loss caused by the establishment of facilitates provided for in the paragraph 2 or to the person who suffered a loss arising from the inability of obtaining the permission provided for in paragraph 5.

The amount of the compensation provided for in the preceding paragraph shall be decided by the Director-General of the Environment Agency or the prefectural governor.

The person who is not satisfied with the decision provided for in the preceding paragraph shall claim the increase of the amount of compensation with a suit within three months from the day when he was informed the decision.

In the case of the suit of the preceding paragraph, the State or prefecture shall be a defendant.

Article 9

The prefectural governor, in case when the game is decreased in a given area, and he deems it necessary to increase such game, shall establish a temporary hunting prohibited area in the period of not more than three years.

Article 10

The prefectural governor, when he deems it necessary for prevention of danger and others, may establish the gun hunting prohibited area.

Malawi

Article 26

(1) For the purposes of this Act, there shall be declared protected areas of public land to be known as national parks or wildlife reserves.

(2) The declaration and management of national parks and wildlife reserve shall be subject to the provisions of sections 27 to 41.

Article 28

(1) The Minister may, by order published in the Gazette, declare any area of land or water within Malawi to be a national park or to be a wildlife reserve and may, in like manner, alter the boundaries of, or disestablish, any national park or wildlife reserve so declared, and the Minister shall first require the matter to be comprehensively studies by or under the auspices of the Board.

(2) The Minister may amend such order, but any order the purpose of which is to alienate or excise land from a

national park or wildlife reserve shall be of no effect unless and until approved by a resolution of the National Assembly.

(3) Any study made pursuant to the provision of subsection (1) shall investigate the ecological consequences of the proposed boundary change or disestablishment, and the report of the study shall be submitted to the Minister together with the advice of the Board within ninety days of the study being made.

(4) The Minister shall not decide upon any proposal relating to boundary change or disestablishment of any national park or wildlife reserve until he is in receipt of a report made pursuant to subsection (3).

PROCEDURE FOR ACQUISITION OF LAND

Bulgaria

Article 9

1. Upon increasing of size or inclusion of new protected areas in the Annexes under Article 8, paragraph 1, the forests, lands and aquatic areas owned by the natural and legal persons, and the privately owned by municipalities shall be expropriated following the procedures of the State Property Act.
2. Except for the cases under paragraph 1, the declaration of protected areas shall not change the ownership of forests, lands and aquatic areas therein.

Canada

Acquisition of Lands

Article 9

(1) The Governor in Council may authorize the Minister to purchase, acquire or lease any lands or interests therein for the purpose of research, conservation and

interpretation in respect of (a) migratory birds; or (b) with the agreement of the government of the province having an interest therein, other wildlife.

Restrictions

(2) Lands or interests therein purchased or acquired pursuant to subsection (1) shall not be disposed of, and no person shall use or occupy the lands, except under the authority of this Act or the regulations.

Sale or Lease of Lands

(3) The Minister may authorize the sale, lease or other disposition of lands purchased or acquired pursuant to subsection (1) if, in the opinion of the Governor in Council, the sale, leasing or other disposition is compatible with wildlife research, conservation and interpretation.

Japan

Article 8-2

The State or prefecture shall compensate the loss to be occurred naturally to the person who suffered a loss caused by the establishment of facilitates provided for in the paragraph 2 or to the person who suffered a loss arising from the inability of obtaining the permission provided for in paragraph 5.

The amount of the compensation provided for in the preceding paragraph shall be decided by the Director-General of the Environment Agency or the prefectural governor.

Malawi

Section 29

Any area of land proposed for national park or wildlife reserve status and which is not public land shall first be acquired as public land in accordance with the provisions of the Land Act and Lands Acquisition Act.

ADMINISTRATIVE PROVISIONS

Bulgaria

Article 78

To prevent and discontinue administrative violations hereof and there harmful consequences, the competent authorities or persons authorised by them shall impose compulsory administrative measures in accordance with Article 80-79.

Article 79

1. The Minister of Environment and Waters shall cancel:

   (i) orders of central authorities that contravene this Act or do not comply with the established protected area regimens.

   (ii) the implementation of development and technical plans and projects approved in violation hereof.

2. The Directors of the regional authorities of the Ministry of Environment and Waters shall.

   (i) cancel uses of forests, lands and aquatic areas, and other resources as well as construction within the protected areas that are in violation of properly approved management plans, development plans and technical plans and projects, or are not agreed under the procedures hereunder in the absence of such plans and projects;

   (ii) cancel activities or sites which damage or that pollute the environment within the protected areas in excess of the admissible levels;

   (iii) cancel orders of the Regional Directorates of Forests, Forestry Enterprises and municipal authorities that are in violation hereof or of the protected area regimens;

   (iv) issue prescriptions for measures to prevent and remove the harmful consequences of admitted violations or environmental damage and pollution within protected areas.

3. The directors of the Regional Directorates of Forests, and of the Forestry Enterprises and the Mayors of Municipalities shall cancel activities and construction within forests, lands and aquatic areas submitted for use within state, municipality or privately owned protected areas, if performed in violation of the approved management plans and development and technical plans and projects.

Article 80

The compulsory administrative measures can be appealed against through the channels established in the Administrative Procedures Act.

POWERS OF THE MINISTER

3. The Minister May

(a) undertake, promote and recommend measures for the encouragement of public cooperation in wildlife conservation and interpretation;
(b) initiate conferences and meetings respecting wildlife research, conservation and interpretation;
(c) undertake programs for wildlife research and investigation, and establish and maintain laboratories and other necessary facilities for that purpose;
(d) establish such advisory committees as the Minister deems necessary and appoint the members of those committees; and
(e) coordinate and implement wildlife policies and programs in cooperation with the government of any province having an interest therein.

China

Article 30

The administrative measures for wildlife under special local protection and for other wildlife that is not under special state protection shall be formulated by the standing committees of the people's congresses of provinces, autonomous regions and municipalities directly under the Central Government.

Malawi

Section 5

For the purpose of implementing this Act, there snail be appointed in the public service an officer to be designated as the Chief Parks and Wildlife Officer and other officers subordinate to him who shall be responsible for the administration of this Act subject to any general or special directions of the Minister.

Section 6

(1) The Chief Parks and Wildlife Officer shall, subject to the general or special directions of the Minister, be responsible for the management of national parks and wildlife throughout Malawi and, in particular, for implementing the provisions of this Act, and shall exercise control over national parks and wildlife reserves in accordance with the provisions of this Act and any order declaring a national park or a wildlife reserve.

(2) Every officer shall exercise such functions and duties as may be conferred upon him by this Act or as may be delegated or assigned to him by the Chief Parks and Wildlife Officer.

Section 19

The function of the Board shall be to advise the Minister on all matters relating to national parks and wildlife management in Malawi, including in particular but not limited to—

(a) advising on the declaration of areas which, for the purpose of protecting wildlife species, biotic communities, sites of species interest or aesthetic values, the Board considers should be declared national parks or wildlife reserves under this Act; and

(b) advising on the import, export and re-export of wildlife specimens into and out of Malawi.

PENAL PROVISIONS

Bulgaria

Section II : Administrative Violations and Sanctions

Article 81

1. Fines of 500,000 to 25,000,000 levis shall be imposed on natural persons who:

    1. realizes perform activities in the protected area in violation of the regime determined with this Act, the declaration order or approved management plans and projects under Chapter Four;
    2. perform activities within the protected area without the permission provided for herein.

2. When the activity under paragraph 1, items 1 and 2 is construction, the fine shall amount to 5,000,000 to 20,000,000 levis, and when the activity is for development of areas, the fine shall amount to 2,000,000 to 20,000,000 levis.
3. In unimportant minor cases under paragraph 1, when no damage to the protected area has been caused, the fine shall be 5,000 to 1200,000 levis.

Article 82

1. Fines of 500,000 to 10,000,000 levis shall be imposed on officials who:

    1. allow or order, or fail to impose penalties for activities or construction within a protected area in violation of the regimen set forth herein, in the declaration order or in the approved management plans and development and technical plans and projects under Chapter Four.

2. do not agree with the competent authorities upon activities within a protected area without approved plans and projects under Chapter Four.

Article 83

1. Fines or, respectively, property sanctions from 1,000,000 to 510,000,000 levis shall be imposed to sole traders or natural legal persons who:

   1. realizes perform activities in protected areas in violation of the regime determined with this Act, with the declaration order or approved management plans and projects under Chapter Four;
   2. perform activities within the protected area without the permission provided for herein;

2. When the activity under paragraph 1, items 1 and 2 is construction or development of areas, the fine shall amount to 5,000,000 to 50,000,000 levis;
3. In unimportant minor cases under paragraph 1, the fine shall be 100,000 to 1,000,000 levis.

Article 84

1. The objects that constitute the violation and the objects used in committing thereof within protected areas that are exclusive property of the state, shall be expropriated to the benefit of the state.
2. The procedure for the sale of the objects under paragraph 1 shall be set forth in a Regulation of the Council of Ministers.

Article 85

1. The violations under Articles 82, 81 and 84, 83 shall be established with a writ issued by an official person nominated by the Minister of Environment and Waters,

the Minister of Agriculture, Forests and Agrarian Reform, or by the Mayor of the Municipality. The penal ordinances shall be issued, respectively, by the Minister of Environment and Waters, the Minister of Agriculture, Forests and Agrarian Reform and the mayor of the municipality or by persons authorised by them.

2. The violations under Articles 83, 82 shall be established by means of a writs issued by an officials person nominated by the Minister of Environment and Waters, and the penal ordinances shall be issued by the Minister of Environment and Waters or by persons authorized by him/her.
3. The establishment of violations, issuance, appealing and amendment forcing of penal ordinances shall be made following the procedures of the Administrative Violations and Penalties Act.

Article 86

1. For damages caused to protected areas, the guilty persons shall pay compensation based on a tariff adopted by the Councilor Ministers but not less than the amount of the damage.
2. The amounts collected under paragraph 1 shall be transferred into:

    1. The National Environmental Protection Fund, when the penal ordinances are issued by officials from the system of the Ministry of Environment and Waters.
    2. The Bulgarian Forest Fund when the penal ordinances are issued by officials from the system of the Ministry of Agriculture, Forests and Agrarian Reform.
    3. The relevant municipal fund when the penal ordinances are issued by officials of the municipalities.

3. If the violation has been committed by a third person

within properties or sites owned by natural or legal persons, the compensation shall be determined to the benefit of the relevant owner.

4. If the violation has been committed by the owner of the property or the site, the compensation shall be transferred to the National Environmental Protection Fund.

Canada

Contravention of Act or Regulations

13. (1) Every person who contravenes subsection 11 (6) or any regulation.

(a) is guilty of an offence punishable on summary conviction and is liable :

 (i) in the case of a corporation, to a fine not exceeding $100,000, and
 (ii) in the case of an individual, to a fine not exceeding $50,000 or to imprisonment for a term not exceeding six months, or to both; or

(b) is guilty of an indictable offence and is liable :

 (i) in the case of a corporation, to a fine not exceeding $250,000, and
 (ii) in the case of an individual, to a fine not exceeding $100,000 or to imprisonment for a term not exceeding five years, or to both.

Subsequent Offence

(2) Where a person is convicted of an offence under this Act a second or subsequent time, the amount of the fine for the subsequent offence may, notwithstanding subsection (1), be double the amount set out in that subsection.

Continuing Offence

(3) A person who commits or continues an offence on more

than one day is liable to be convicted for a separate offence for each day on which the offence is committed or continued.

Fines Cumulative

(4) A fine imposed for an offence involving more than one animal, plant or other organism may be calculated in respect of each one as though it had been the subject of a separate information and the fine then imposed is the total of that calculation.

Additional Fine

(5) Where a person has been convicted of an offence and the court is satisfied that monetary benefits accrued to the person as a result of the commission of the offence,

(a) the court may order the person to pay an additional fine in an amount equal to the court's estimation of the amount of the monetary benefits; and

(b) the additional fine may exceed the maximum amount of any fine that may otherwise be imposed under this Act.

China

Article 31

Anyone who illegally catches or kills wildlife under special state protection shall be prosecuted for criminal responsibility in accordance with the supplementary provisions on punishing the crimes of catching or killing the species of wildlife under special state protection which are rare or near extinction.

Article 32

If anyone, in violation of the provisions of this Law, hunts or catches wildlife in an area or during a season closed to hunting or uses prohibited hunting gear or methods for the purpose, his catch, hunting gear and unlawful income shall be confiscated and he shall be fined by the department of wildlife administration; if the circumstances are serious enough to constitute a crime, he shall be prosecuted for criminal responsibility in accordance with the provisions of Article 130 of the Criminal Law.

Article 33

If anyone, in violation of the provisions of this Law, hunts or catches wildlife without a hunting license or in violation of the prescriptions of the hunting license, his catch and unlawful income shall be confiscated and he shall be fined by the department of wildlife administration and, in addition, his hunting gear may be confiscated and his hunting license revoked.

If anyone, in violation of the provisions of this Law, hunts wildlife with a hunting rifle without a license for the rifle, he shall be punished by a public security organ by applying mutatis mutandis the provisions of the Regulations on Administrative Penalties for Public Security.

Article 34

If anyone, in violation of the provisions of this Law, destroys in nature reserves or areas closed to hunting the main places where wildlife under special state or local protection lives and breeds, he shall be ordered by the department of wildlife administration to stop his destructive acts and restore these places to their original state within a prescribed time limit, and shall be fined.

Article 35

If anyone, in violation of the provisions of this Law, sells, purchases, transports or carries wildlife under special state or local protection or the products thereof, such wildlife and products and his unlawful income shall be confiscated by the administrative authorities for industry and commerce and he may concurrently be fined.

If anyone, in violation of the provisions of this Law, sells or purchases wildlife under special state protection or the products thereof, and if the circumstances are serious enough to constitute a crime of speculation or smuggling, he shall be prosecuted for criminal responsibility according to the relevant provisions of the Criminal Law.

The wildlife or the products thereof thus confiscated shall, in accordance with the relevant provisions, be disposed of by the relevant department of wildlife administration or by a unit authorized by the same department.

Article 36

If anyone illegally imports or exports wildlife or the products thereof, he shall be punished by the Customs according to the Customs Law; if the circumstances are serious enough to constitute a crime, he shall be prosecuted for criminal responsibility in accordance with the provisions of the Criminal Law on the crimes of smuggling.

Article 37

If anyone forges, sells or re-sells or transfers a special hunting and catching license, a hunting license, a domestication and breeding license, or an import or export permit, his license or permit shall be revoked and his unlawful income shall be confiscated and he may concurrently be fined by the relevant department of wildlife administration or the administrative authorities for industry and commerce.

If anyone who forges or sells or re-sells a special hunting and catching license or an import or export permit, and if the circumstances are serious enough to constitute a crime, he shall be prosecuted for criminal responsibility by applying mutatis mutandis the provisions of Article 167 of the Criminal Law.

Japan

Article 21

Any person shall be liable to a penal servitude less than one year or a fine of not more than fifty thousand yen in any of the following cases:

If he has contravened the provisions of Articles 3, 11, 15, 16 or 20-2;
If he has made hunting in a gun hunting prohibited area;
If he has received by fraudulence the hunting permit or such permission as referred to in Article 12, paragraph 1;

Any thing used for criminal purpose violating the provisions of items (1) or (2) of the preceding paragraph as well as any game taken through other crimes and owned by criminal shall be forfeited.

Article 22

Any person shall be subject to a penal servitude less than six months or a fine of not more than thirty thousand yen in any of the following cases:

- If he has contravened the provisions of Article 1-4 paragraph 1, Article 2, Article 4 paragraph 7, Article 13, Article 13-2, or Article 20;

  If he has failed to abide by any prohibition or restrictions under Articles 1-4 paragraph 3;

  If he has let others use his own hunting license, the permit under the provision of Article 12 paragraph 2, or the raising permit under the provision of Article 13;

  If he has used other's hunting license, the permit under the provision of Article 12 paragraph 2 or the raising permit under the provision of Article 13.

Article 22-2

Any person who has contravened the provision of Article 8-2 paragraph 2 or 5, Article 17 or 18 shall be liable to a fine of not more than thirty thousand yen provided that any criminal in violation of the provision of Article 17 shall be indicated upon complaint of either occupant or any license-holder for joint game area.

Article 23

Any person shall be liable to a fine of not more than ten thousand yen in any of the following cases:

If he has contravened. the provision of Article 14 paragraph 3 or Article 19;

If he has refused, obstructed or evaded such inspection by entering as provided for in the provision of Article 19-2 paragraph 1;

If he has failed to submit report in accordance with the provision of Article 20-3 or made false report;

If he has moved, damaged, wrecked or removed any sign of sanctuary, special sanctuary, temporary hunting prohibited area, or any facilities as referred to in the provision of Article 8-2, paragraph 2;

Article 24

In case where any person who had received a hunting permit or the permit under the provision of Article 12 paragraph 1 has been sentenced a penalty more than a fine by contravening the provision of this law or the ordinance of the Prime Minister's Office or the regulation of prefecture issued there under, his hunting license or the permit shall become null and void.

Article 25

In case where any representative of a juridical person or any proxy, employee or other worker of a juridical or natural person has acted in violation of the provisions of Articles 21 to 23 inclusive with respect to business of the juridical or natural person, the latter shall also be liable to the punishment inflicted on the real offender, unless it is proved that due care and supervision has been exercised in connection with the business of said juridical or natural person in order to prevent such violation by the proxy, employee, or other worker thereof.

Malawi

Section 110

Any person who is convicted of an offence involving :

(a) taking, hunting, molesting, or reducing into possession any protected species other than game species; or

(b) possession of, selling, buying, transferring or accepting in transfer any specimen of protected species other than game species;

(c) contravention of sections 32, 33, and 35 of this Act, shall be liable to a fine of K10,000 and to imprisonment for a term of 5 years, and in any case the fine shall not be less than the value of the specimen involved in the commission of the offence.

Section 111

Any person who is convicted of an offence under section 98 or under regulations made pursuant to section 99 shall be liable to a fine of K 10,000 and to imprisonment for a term of 5 years, and in any case the fine shall not be less than the value of the specimen involved in the commission of the offence.

Section 112

If any person is convicted of an offence under this Act in respect of any excavation, fence, enclosure or any other device fixed in or on the ground or upon vegetation, which the person has made, used or had in his possession for the purpose of hunting in contravention of this Act, the court shall, in addition to any other penalty imposed, order the device to be destroyed or obliterated in such manner as the court may specify, and any expenditure incurred, if any, shall be recoverable from the person as a civil debt owed to the Government.

OBSERVATION

(1) Authority

Through above study of this point as authorities is describe in section or Article of the respective Country. I have also observed during my study on this very same topic the term China—forestry and fishery are under two ministerial levels in Japan we have come across authority as Perfectural Governor and Directorial General of Environmental agency.

Yet, he is called chief and wild life officer in the parks and wild life in Malawi there chief and the wild life officer have their subordinate under them, commonly called has been differentiate in Canada and China as Ministers. He is given a different name like in Bulgaria Park director and Regional Inspector are the name given to this authority that looks after the system.

In India authorities are discussed in Sections 3 to 8 of the Chapter-II of the Wild Life (Protection) Act, 1972.

(2) Ownership

In Bulgaria Parks are the exclusive property of the State that include plant and animal species my observation in Canada no where has it been described in particular the land which is to be passed by the wildlife (Public land is within the Jurisdiction/ name of her majesty).

Coming to China, it is inherent in Article 3 that wildlife resources are the property of the State.

In Japan, I have not come across any such provision, which states the ownership of the wild life.

In Malawi it is stated in section 4 of Part I that the complete land, which pertains to wild animal and wild plant, is vested in the possession of president.

In India this right of ownership of the land for the wild life is vested in the hand of the sovereign, which is the State.

Thus it is not wrong to observe that out of six countries only two i.e. Canada and Japan have not mentioned specifically in their respective Wildlife Act.

(3) Categories of Protected Areas

In Bulgaria their are 6 categories of the protected areas which have been described namely: Strict Nature Reserve, National Park, Natural Monument, Menaged Reserve, Natural Park and Protected site. In Canada no specific mention of the area is give beet on the contrary the procedure for the protection of wild life has given.

In China Two Categories of Protected area have given i.e. nature reserves and areas closed to hunting and during seasons closed to hunting the hunting and catching of wild life and other activities which are have full to living and breeding wild life.

In India this aspect is dealt in sections 18, 35 and 37 of the Wild Life (Protection) Act, 1972.

Here too excepting Canada all countries of my study have described this Category of the protected areas.

(4) Declaration of Protected Areas

It is observed that every country has the provision regarding the Declaration of the Protected Areas accept that of Canada. Where I could not find any specific mention in this regard. As far as India is concerned there is a provision laid down under Sections 26A, 35, 37 of the Wild Life (Protection) Act, 1972.

(5) Procedure of Acquisition of Land

In Bulgaria, China and Japan there is no specific mention of Completion acquisition of land for the wild life though the protected areas have been mentioning this regard. In Canada it is specifically mention in Article 9 (1) that Governor in Council may authorize the minister to purchases, acquire or lease any lands or interests therein for the purpose of research, conservation and interpretation in respects of migratory birds.

In Malawi section 29 says that any land for the national park or wild life reserve when is not public land, shall first be acquired as public land in accordance with the provision of the land Act and Lands Acquisition Act.

In India acquisition of rights are discussed in Section 25 and acquisition of proceeding are mentioned in Section 25 of the Wild Life (Protection) Act, 1972.

(6) Administrative Provisions

In Bulgaria chapter six of protected areas law 1998 deals with administrative and penal provisions this chapter is divided into two section in which Chapter I deals with the compulsory administrative measures which spread from Articles 78, 79 and 80 Article 78 talks of the prevention and discontinuous administrative violation and them harmful consequence and administrative authorities and person authorised for them shall be compulsory administrative provision with Articles 79, 80 the appeal against the administrative measures can be done so through the channels established in the administrative procedure Act.

In Canada the Administration has been given in the lands of minister who has to undertake, promote and recommend measure for the encouragement of public corporation in wild life conservation and Interpretation they have to undertake the programmes research and investigation, establish and maintain library for this purpose they also have to establish advisory committee as he deems necessary. He has to coordinate, implement the wild life policies and programme in the cooperation with the government of any provisions have interest therein.

In China Article 30 deals with the Administration provision for the wild life for the special local and State Protection this is formulated by the standing committee of the people congress of the provinces, autonomous region, municipalities and the central government.

In Japan Articles 1-2 says that the Perfectural Governor will have to abide by the Standard Specified by the Director General of the Environment agency upon hearing the opinion of the Nature Conservation Council.

In this part he has to provide certain specifications like the term of the tenure, matters regarding establishing of sanctuaries, provision regarding Temporary hunting in prohibiting area etc. He has to look into the matter regarding artificial propagation of game, survey of habitat of the game, public information, development of steps to workout the game, protection project and other necessary matter for execution of game project.

In Malawi Section 5 of Malawi National Parks and Wild Life Act (1992) tells us that then has to be one officer designation as Chief Park and wild life officer and some subordinate officer will be responsible for administrative subject to any general and special direction given by the minister.

Article 6.1 says that it is the minister who is responsible for the National Park and wild life in the country of Malawi it is also observed that every officer shall exercise such duty is confirm upon their in the Act of us may delegate or assign him by the Chief, park and wild life officer. It is does not go without notice that there is a board which is set-up to active the Minister to all matter relating to national Park and wild life management in Malawi. It is through board consideration and recommendation the import and export; export of wild life into or out Malawi is done.

In India this provision is vastly dealt in various heads like the sanctuaries, the parks etc. The looking after of these wildlife are done under the supervision of the Collector and the Chief Wildlife Warden.

(7) Penal Provision

My observations will not be completed without specific mention of the sanctions/punishment given to those persons who have violated any law, which are made for the protection, administration and looking after these wild lives and sanctuaries. Bulgaria has this provision Under Section 2 under Article 81 of Act.

Article 85 further says that any violation done under Articles 82, 83, 84 shall be established with a writ issued by an official. The penal ordinances issued by different minister and officer or authorised person. Section 2 of Article 85 says a violation of Article 83 or 82 will be punishable by official person nominated by Minister. Appeal laid down in Section 3 of Article 85 would be under the procedure Act.

Article 85 further highlights that the damages cost to protected areas, the guilty one has to paid compensation based on a tariff adopted by the Councilor Minister not less than the amount of damages.

The punishment money (amount collected is segregated amongst the Environmental fund, forest fund and Municipal fund. Violations, which has been committed by their person, the compensation shall be determined for the benefit of the relevant owner. If the violation has been committed by the owner the compensation shall be transferred to the environmental fund.

Coming to Canada, here also punishment for the wrong doer the punishment levied upon him would be as follows:

(i) in case of corporation fine dose not exceed $ 100,000 and in case of individual it does not exceed $ 50,000 or imprisonment for a term not exceeding 6 months or both.

(ii) Guilty of an indetectable offence, here the punishment in case of corporation does not exceed $ 250,000 and in case of individual does not exceed $ 100,000 or the imprisonment not exceeding 5 years or both. There is a punishment for continuing offence as well as that if a person continues on doing the offence more than one day is liable to be convicted for a separate offence for each day on which the offence has been committed.

Fines are seen to be cumulative i.e. where the offence evolves more than one animal or plant may be calculated and the some total of the amount is levied upon the accused, but where the court is not satisfied with the amount of monitory, fine may be added by order the additional amount on which there is an amount equal to the courts estimation amount of monitory benefit this additional fund (fine money) may exceed the maximum amount of any fine that may be otherwise imposed under this provision of the Act.

Coming to China Article 31 says that anyone who illegally catches or harms or kills the wild life comes under the special State protection.

It further says that if the circumstances are serious enough to constitute a crime, he shall be prosecuted for criminal responsibility in accordance with the provision of the Article 130 of the criminal law.

Similarly Articles 33, 34, 35, 36 and 37 all deal with the punishment.

Japan here also a wrong doer does not getaway without servitude less than one year or fines not more than 30,000 Yen in any of the following cases which are given 3, 11, 15, 16 or 222.

Similarly Articles 23, 24, 25 also gave different punishment to the wrong doer.

In Malawi all the punishment, which are levied upon the wrong doer, is recovered as a civil death owned to the government.

In India the sanction provision is laid down in the name of prevention and detention of offences. Which are given Under Section 50 to 58 of the Wild Life (Protection) Act, 1972.

(8) Settlement of Tribal Rights

As our study is mostly concerned with the right of Tribal. To my amazing surprise I could not find any specific right of Tribal People in any of the above discussed countries. But in India there is this mention that the Tribals will be compensated after their lands have been taken away from them by the State in form of either settling them in a different places and making arrangements for them, for ploughing of their lands.

Notes and References

1. R.S. Bedi and A.S. Bedi, Encyclopaedia of Environment and Pollution Laws (Delhi: Orient Law House), 2002, Page 1302.
2. http://www.iisd.ca/download/asc/sd/sdvo/89numl.txt
3. http://www.iisd.ca/download/asc/sd/sdvo/89numl.txt
4. http://www.iisd.ca/download/asc/sd/sdvo/89numl.txt
5. R.S. Bedi and A.S. Bedi 1303.
6. R.S. Bedi and A.S. Bedi 1305.
7. R.S. Bedi and A.S. Bedi 1305.
8. R.S. Bedi and'A.S. Bedi 1310.
9. R.S. Bedi and A.S. Bedi 1309.

10. R.S. Bedi and A.S. Bedi 1311.
11. R.S. Bedi and A.S. Bedi 1322.
12. R.S. Bedi and A.S. Bedi 1328.
13. R.S. Bedi and A.S. Bedi 1322.
14. Justice Ashoka A. Desai, ·Environmental Jurisprudence, (Allahabad: Modem Law House, 2002) 340.
15. R.S. Bedi and A.S. Bedi 1380.
16. Dr. S.K. Kapoor, International Law and Human Rights (Allahabad: Central Law Agency, 2002) 416.
17. http://www:mma.gov. br/port/sbf/reuniao/doc/finaldoc. pdf
18. http://www.iucn.org
19. http://www.iucn.org
20. http://www.iucn.org

Indian Laws to Protect the Wild Life : Comparative Observations

Chapter 1 concentrates on the international measures, which have been adopted by different international organisations and countries for the protection of wild life. No doubt these measures are important as the theme of most of the national laws is derived from these international measures. But this does not dilute the significance of the national laws as international treaties and declarations are only directives. The Sovereign States are directed but not bound by it unless and until they are recognised and rectified by them in the form of national laws.

India adopted Wild Life (Protection) Act, 1972 on the basis of the principles laid down in the Stockholm Declaration (1972) and declared many areas as National Parks and Sanctuaries for the protection of wild life.

HISTORY OF NATIONAL PARKS AND SANCTUARIES

Many countries have developed conservation legislation and institutions for conservation of the natural resources. More than 3000 national parks and protected areas are now being maintained in well over 400 million habitats in 90 percent of the world's biogeographically regions.

Earlier protected areas were established to serve the recreational and hunting needs of the blue blooded royal people. This object of declaring the protected areas continued till the World War II.

After World War II philosophy of recreation changed and new concept of conservation was born. This conservation included ecological balance or biological diversity. Reasons for worldwide conservation movement can be attributed to the loss of biological diversity, imbalanced ecosystem and the degradation of habitats. Various efforts have been and are being made, both at the international and national level to envisage this conservation movement.

After ruthless exploitation of natural resources developed and developing countries have realised the importance of conservation for the sustainable development of human society. The developed countries advocated for the conservation of wild life. Various efforts have been made for balancing the ecosystem so far. The developed countries encouraged the less developed or developing countries for conservation by giving them financial and technical assistance. This is an important reason for which, the governments of various developing countries have taken the initiatives to create, more national parks and sanctuaries. The developing countries have been bringing in more and more land under national parks and sanctuaries but have ignored its social, cultural, economical and political conditions.

National parks and protected areas constitute substantial part of world land. Since 1950, there has been a marked growth in the number of national parks and sanctuaries. Automatically a crucial question arises that what are the reasons for vigorous growth of such protected areas? What are the political or economic obligations created by the developed countries? Does this conservation policy prove beneficiary for economic and cultural growth of the country?

WILD LIFE CONSERVATION IN INDIA—A BRIEF HISTORY

After having glimpse of the various international measures for the conservation of wild life let us come down to discuss the measures for the conversation of wild life in India. Conservation of wild life includes "preservation of all species the enhancement of wild life habitat, the control of wild life problems, and the consumptive use of wildlife."[1] India being a country richly endowed with a wide variety of fauna and flora is worlds richest country in bio-diversity and natural wealth.

> With a forest cover of 19 percent of its total geographical area of which as much as 11 percent is good or dense forest, India is home to 372 mammals 1228 birds, 428 reptiles, 204 amphibians, 2546 fishes, 57, 245 insects, 5,042 molluscses and several other species of invertebrates. It is the only country to have all the five major vertebrates—the tiger, lion, panther, elephant and the rhino. Of the 81,000 species of animals recorded.[2]

For suitable conservation of biological diversity, India has developed a protected area network of 1.53 lac sq. mts. comprising 86 national parks and 480 wild life sanctuaries.

Traditional Conservation

Conservation of forests and wild life is not new for India. Despite vast population, civilization and industrialisation we have better wild life heritage because of our traditional conservation policies. The Indian tradition of wild life conservation goes back to the Vedic period and has been continuing till now. 22 centuries ago Emperor Ashoka gave emphasis on conservation of forests. Writings and pictures on the iron pillars of that time provide substantive evidence for it. He made it the King's duty to preserve animal's life and trees. Indus valley civilization also had respect, love and affection for nature Elephant; rhino image speaks about the sense of human love for wild life at that time. Our old epic like the Ramayana, the Mahabharata have also emphasised on the importance of animals.

Less than 200 years ago, the need to protect wild life was normally perceived solely in human terms, such as the desirability of preserving game quarry species and the protected areas were the few places, where we could find them. There is little doubt that an incidental benefit of this human centred approach was the protection of other animals and plants and the preservation of the whole area in a natural state. But there were few laws designed specifically to protect the wild life.

The history of evolution of species has put man on the apex only through the wild life. Traversing through the animal breed, man claims today to be on the summit of civilisation. The progress of mankind has been largely inspired by the conduct of the beasts. In the Brithadaranyak Upnishad, the first espousal couple, Manu and Shatrupa, are described to have learnt the procreative art through the fornication among sheep and rams among cows and the oxen, among mares and horses. Three out of the five attributes of a scholar (काक चेष्टा बकोध्यानम् श्वान निद्रा तदैव चः। अल्पहारी, ब्रह्मचारी विद्यार्थीनाम् पंच लक्षणे।।) namely rolling like a crow, meditation like the hornbill, sleep like a dog have been adopted from the conduct of animals or birds in addition to the other two, namely, celibacy and dieting. The male and the female crane are adored as the ideal couple. The eagle for its eyesight, the vixen for its cleverness and the crocodile for its tears, are well known. The moral is to accept in life the virtues, and abhor the evil tendencies of these species.

From time immemorial animals have also been a potential source of useful articles for man like musk, bees wax, honey, lac, silk, pearl, etc. Rigveda emphasises the importance of plants and animals and even the Upanishads have provision for ecological balance. The earliest codified laws pertaining to wild life in India can be traced back to the 3rd century B.C., when Ashoka, the King of Magadha enacted a law related to the preservation of wild life and environment.

The importance of preserving trees and forest is not a new phenomenon for India History tells us that ancient administrators of our country understood the importance of wild life and ecological balance. Arthasastra stresses the need to preserve forests and elephant population. Chatrapati Shivaji during his reign banned the cutting of trees.

British period in India can be traced back 1600 A.D. when East India Company came to India. There were no codified laws for wild life protection. In those times every province had their own laws, (local laws). In Hindu reign it was Hindu law, which prevailed and in the Muslim reign it was Muslim law.

After 1800 A.D. Britishers laid the foundation of scientific forest management in India. Before that the land was divided in two categories the waste land i.e., the forestland and the Revenue land (the land left for the use of people).

Codification of law for the administration of forests started from the year 1865. First codified law on forest came in to existence in the Statute book, and was known as the Indian Forest Act VII of 1865, subsequently, this was replaced by the Indian Forest Act VII of 1878 which, was further amended in the year 1890, 1901, 1918, 1919, and finally in the year 1927 which is still in existence. The forest Act of 1878 ensured that the reservation of forests did not affect the existing rights of individuals or communities.

There are some other regional laws for the Protection of Wild life like: The Madras Act for prevention of the indiscriminate destruction of Wild Elephants, Elephants Preservation Act of 1879, Tamil Nadu (Preservation of Wild Elephants) Act of 1878, The Wild Life Birds Protection Act, 1887. This Act enabled the government to form rules prohibiting the possession or sale of specific wild birds, which have been killed or caged during the breeding season.

Until now laws relating to the protection of wild life were limited to provinces or regions. It was only in 1912 when a unified law was passed for the first time for the country (India). In 1912 with the promulgation of the Wild Birds and Animals Protection Act came the first comprehensive legislation for control and management of Wild animals including its habitat. This act of 1912 was amended in 1935 by the wild Birds and Animals Protection (Amendment) Act, 1935 (27 of 1935). All these laws essentially aimed at prevention of hunting or game of animals, and prohibition of trade of animal's organs or products made by them.

Forest Act of 1865 had provisions for regulation of forest exploitation, management and preservation. It also laid stress on people's customary rights over forests and forest produce. This Act was only applicable to the forest of government but had not included private forests.

The Forest Act of 1865 was further amended by the Forest Act of 1878. By this Act, Forest came under the control of the State and gradually the control of the government on the forests increased. For the first time certain acts were declared forest offences and were punishable. The Act also had some provisions for the private forests.

It was only in 1927 when an attempt was made to codify all the laws of the forest. The legislation laid emphasis on the exploitation of the forests, for revenue purposes rather than on the values of preservation or conservation. This is evident from the Preamble of Forest Act, 1927 which stated that: An Act to consolidate the law relating to forests, the transit of forest produce and the duty leviable on timber and other forest produce. The areas which are declared Protected Areas under Wild Life Protection Act are those areas which are declared reserve forests or protected forests under Indian Forest Act. To quote the Provisions of Indian Forests Act I have consulted the book *Environmental Law* by I.A. Khan. This Act placed the forests in three categories. This Act placed the forests in three categories of the forest, Reserve Forest, Village Forest and the Protected Forest Chapter II of the Indian Forest Act, 1927 deals with the reserved forests.

Power to Reserve Forests

The State Government may constitute any forest land or wasteland which is the property of Government, or over which the Government has proprietary rights, or to the whole or any part of the forest produce of , which the Government is entitled a reserved forest.[1]

Bar of Accrual of Forest Rights: After the issue of a notification under section 4, no right shall be acquired. . . in or over the land comprised in such notification, except by succession or under a grant or contract in writing made or entered into by or on behalf of the Government or some person in whom such right was vested when the notification was issued; and no fresh clearings for cultivation or for any other purpose shall be made in such land except in accordance with such rules as may be made by the State Government in this behalf.[2]

Extinction of Rights

Rights in respect of which no claim has been preferred under section 6, and of the existence of which no knowledge has been acquired by inquiry under section 7, shall be extinguished,

1. Section 3 of Forest Act 1927.
2. Section 5 of Indian Forest Act, 1927.

unless before the notification under section 20 is published, the person claiming them satisfies the forest Settlement officer that he had sufficient cause for not preferring such claim within the period fixed under section 6.[3]

Exercise of Rights Admitted

(1) After making such record the Forest Settlement officer shall, to the best of his ability, having due regard to the maintenance of the reserved forest in respect of which the claim is made, pass such orders as will ensure the continued exercise of the rights so admitted.

(2) For this purpose the Forest Settlement officer may—

(a) set out some other forest tract of sufficient extent, and in a locality reasonably convenient, for the purposes of such claimants, and record an order conferring upon them a right of pasture or to forest produce (as the case may be) to the extent so admitted; or

(b) so alter the limits of the proposed forest as to exclude forest-land of sufficient extent, and in a locality reasonably convenient, for the purpose of the claimants; or

(c) Record an order, continuing to such claimants a right of pasture or to forest produce, as the case may be, to the extent so admitted, at such reasons, within such portions of the proposed forest, and under such rules, as may be made in this behalf by the State Government.[4]

Commutation of Rights

In case the forest settlement officer find it impossible, having due regard to the maintenance of the reserved forest, to make such settlement under section 15, as shall ensure the continued exercise of the said rights to the extent so admitted, he shall, subject to such rules as the State Government may make in this behalf, commute such rights, by the payment to such persons of

3. Section 9 of Indian Forest Act, 1927.
4. Section 15 of Indian Forest Act, 1927.

a sum of money in lieu thereof, or by the grant of land, or in such other manner as he thinks fit.[5]

Formation of Village Forests

(1) The State Government may assign to any village community the rights of Government to or over any land, which has been constituted a reserved forest, and may cancel such assignment. All forests so assigned shall be called village-forests.

(2) The State Government may make rules for regulating the management of village forests, prescribing the conditions under which the community to which any such assignment is made may be provided with timber or other forest produce or pasture, and their' duties for the protection and improvement of such forest.

(3) All the provisions of this Act relating to reserved forests shall (so far as they are not inconsistent with the rules so made) apply to village-forests.[6]

Protected Forests

(1) The State Government may, by notification in the Official Gazette, declare the provisions of this Chapter IV applicable to any forest-land or waste-land which is not included in a reserved forest, but which is the property of the Government, or over which the Government has proprietary rights, or to the whole or any part of the forest-produce of which the Government is entitled.

(2) The forest land and wasteland comprised in any such notification shall be called a "protected forest".[7]

Power to Issue Notification Reserving Trees, etc.

The State Government may, by notification in the Official Gazette,—

(a) declare any trees or class of trees in a protected forest to be reserved from a date fixed by the notification;

(b) declare that any portion of such forest specified in the notification shall be closed for such term, not exceeding thirty years, as the State Government thinks fit, and that

5. Section 16 of Indian Forest Act, 1927.
6. Section 28 of Indian Forest Act, 1927.
7. Section 29 of Indian Forest Act, 1927.

the rights of private persons, if any, over such portion shall be suspended during such terms, provided that the remainder of such forest be sufficient, and in a locality reasonably convenient, for the due exercise of the right suspended in the portion so closed; or

(c) prohibit, from a date fixed as aforesaid, the quarrying of stone, or the burning of lime or charcoal, or the collection or subjection to any manufacturing process, or removal of, any forest-produce in any such forest, and the breaking up or clearing for cultivation, for building, for herding cattle or for any other purpose, of any land in any such forest.[8]

Publication of Translation such Notification in Neighbourhood

The Collector shall cause a translation into the local vernacular of every notification issued under section 30 to be affixed in a conspicuous place in every town and village in the neighbourhood of the forest comprised in the notification.[9]

AFTER INDEPENDENCE

After independence, the same policy of Government of India Act, 1935 continued and under the Constitution of India, the forest Subject was included in the State list in the seventh Schedule item 19.

After Independence the Constituent Assembly in the drafted Constitution introduced this subject under the title "Protection of Wild Birds and Wild Animals" and placed it at entry No. 20 in the State list. The State legislatures were given powers to legislate their own law in this connection.

In 1976, 9 major changes took place by the 42nd Amendment in the institution. Of the nine changes one, which is relevant to our research work is that the subject of forest was transferred to the concurrent list from the State list. As a result of this strengthened the power of the center on the forest strengthened. Of the various measures, which the Central Government adopted to protect the remaining population of the

8. Section 30 of Indian Forest Act, 1927.
9. Section 31 of Indian Forest Act, 1927.

endangered species, the most important is the 1972 Indian Wild Life (Protection) Act. In its wake, certain regions were declared as protected areas by notifying them as National Parks and Sanctuaries.

CONSTITUTION OF INDIA

The Constitution of India is the "supreme law of the land".[3] All governmental organs and institutions owe their origin to the Constitution and derive their powers from its provisions.

Each and every law of the country take its validity from the Constitution it self. Our Constitution grants fundamental rights to the person/citizen. Along with these some special provisions are also given to the tribesmen. As our state is a Welfare State the Constitution gives certain directions to the State for the Welfare of its Citizens.

The principles therein laid down are nevertheless fundamental in the governance of the country and it shall be the duty of the State to apply these principles in making law. In pursuance of there directive principles India has made Wild Life Protection Act, 1972 for the protection of Wild Life. Under this Act two categories of protected areas have been made i.e., National Parks and Sanctuaries. There is restriction to movement, to reside or to settle there under the Act.

It is often interpreted in the manner that this Act infringes the fundamental rights of the tribes, which are given to them under Article 19 of the Constitution:

- Article 19(1)(d) All citizens shall have the right to move freely throughout the territory of India.
- 19(1)(e) to reside and settle in any part of the territory of India and
- 19(1)(g) to practice any profession, or to carry on any occupation, trade or business.

The other view is that Wild Life (Protection) Act, 1972 is valid because it comes under the Reasonable Restrictions given in Article 19(2) to (6) of Indian Constitution. To protect or conserve the wild life restricting the movement and settlement within the National Parks and Sanctuaries and prohibition of any products made of animal skin comes under the Reasonable Restrictions given under 19(2) to (6).

Directive Principles of the State Policies

Article 48 directs that the state shall endeavour to organise agriculture and animal husbandry on modern and scientific lines and shall, in particular, take steps for preserving and improving the breeds, and prohibiting the slaughter, of cows and calves and other milk and draught cattle.

Although this Article directly does not deal with wild animals but other animals are under its preview. By the Constitution Forty Second Amendment Act, 1976. S. 10 (w.e.f. 3/10/1977). Article 48A was inserted. According to Article 48A "The State shall endeavour to protect and improve the environment and to safeguard the forest and wild life of the country."

The Wild Life (Protection) Act, 1972, and the Environment (Protection) Act, 1986 are the steps taken under, Article 48A of the Indian Constitution.

Although Directive Principles are only Directives for the State for State policies they are not directly enforceable through courts. This neither dilutes their significance nor the obligation the part of the State to protect the wild life of the country, In some cases Supreme Court suggested that Article 48A should be read with Articles 51 (A)(g), 14, and 21.

Fundamental Duties of the Citizens

Part IV-A of the Constitution of India inserted by the Constitution Forty Second Amendment Act, 1976, S.II. (w.e.f. 3.1.1977) which has provision for fundamental duties of the citizens. According to Article 51 (A)(g): "It shall be the duty of every citizen of India to protect and improve the natural environment including forest, lakes, river and wild life and to have compassion for living creatures."

Indirectly Article 51 (A)(f) which says that "It shall be the duty of every citizen of India to value and preserve the rich heritage of our. composite culture", also impose duty to protect wild life because our culture has moral duty for Wild Life Protection.

Legislative Powers

Seventh Schedule (Art. 246) provides three lists, (i) Union List with 97 entries, (ii) II-List State List with 66 and (iii) III-list Concurrent List with 47 entries.

By the Constitution 42nd (Amendment) Act, 1976 S. 57 (w.e.f. 3.1.1977) "subject forest" inserted in entry 17-A, and "Protection of Wild Life and Birds" inserted in entry 17B. "Prevention of Cruelty to Animals" was already under the entry 17 of the III List.

This Amendment placed the Legislative power on Wild Life in the Concurrent List enabling both the Center and State to legislate. All the State Acts relating to Wild Life were repealed when the Central Legislature passed the Wild Life Protection Act, 1972.

Article 253: Under the Indian Constitution Parliament was conferred with the power to make any law for implementing any treaty, agreement or convention with any other country or countries or even decision made at any international conference. Association or body, this power is limited to implementation of decision and that too for a limited period. Most of the laws have been made Pursuance of this Article.

The Prevention of Cruelty to Animals Act, 1960 (Act No. 59, 1960)

Preamble of the Act says that An Act to prevent the infliction of unnecessary pain or suffering to an animals and for that purpose to amend the law relating to the prevention of cruelty to animals.

Section 2(a) of Act Define "animals" means any living creature other than a human being. This act also defines 'capture' and 'domestic animals'.

Section 3 of Act impose duty on person who having the care or charge of any animal to take all reasonable measure to ensure the well being of such animal and to prevent the infliction upon such animal of unnecessary pain or suffering.

Section 4 of the Act has provision for establishment of Animal Welfare Board.

Functions of the Board are discussed in section 9 of the Act. Some of them are as follows:

Board shall study the law relating to prevention of cruelty to animals. Constantly and give advice to government for amendment in such laws; to improvement of in design of vehicles so as to lesson the burden on draught animals, to design slaughter house, advice on matters relating to the medical care and attention which may proved in animal Hospital and Matter connected with Animal welfare Board shall take such step as it may think fit for veterinary assistance, to encourage by the grant of financial assistance—establishment of pingerpoles rescue homes, animals shelters, sanctuaries and the like. Assistance to animal welfare organization, to impart education in relating to the human treatment of animals, Board may make such Regulations as it may think fit for the administration of its offence and for carrying out its functions.

Section 11 of the Act describes cruelty to animals "if any person treating animals cruelly under sub section (1) of Section II shall be deemed to have committed an offence under this Act.

But Sections 14 to 20 of this Act permit experiments on animals for purpose of advancement of knowledge which will be useful for saving or for prolonging life or for combating any disease, whether of human beings, animals or plants.

One committee can be formed by Government for control and supervision of experiments on animals.

Sections 21 to 27 deals with performing animals: They Restrict exhibition and training of performing animals, which the central Govt. may, notify in official Gazette. There Section also has Provision far Registration far that purpose. Section 28 says: Nothing contained in this Act, shall render it an offence to kill animal in a manner required by the religion of any Community.

Wild Life (Protection) Act, 1972

It was only is the sixties that the concern far the rapidly deleting wild life was brought to the forefront, by various prominent wild lives. After passing of The Prevention of Cruelty to Animals Act, 1960 mast of the acts were declared (crimes against animals. But for the special protection far wild life no laws were there far that purpose Wild Life Protection Act was passed in year 1972. This is the single mast significant statute on wild life protection in India.

Though there were several laws relating to wild life prior to 1972, the WLPA was India's first comprehensive legislation, covering the whale country. Its objectives are primarily three fold:

(a) To farm a uniform legislation far the protection of wild life.

(b) To regulate and central trade in wildlife and products thereof.

(c) To establish a network of protected areas in the farm of national parks and sanctuaries.[4]

Amendment Act 16 of 2003—Statement of Objects and Reasons—The Wild Life (Protection Act) 1972 provides for the protection of wild animals, birds plants. The said Act provides, *inter alia,* for the legal framework for the protection of various species of wild animals, management of their habitats and regulation and control of trade in parts and products derived from various species of wild animals.

2. Taking into consideration the increase in wild life Crimes and growing alienation of local communities from wild life conservation programmes, the Central Government constituted an inter-State committee in the year 1995, comprising representatives from the Central and State Governments, non-governmental organisations and various institutions and experts to review the Wild Life Act with the basic objectives of maintaining and managing the wild life habitats on co-operative and scientific lines as well as effective control of increased poaching and illegal trade of wild life products. The proposed legislation is also needed to provide for scientific and participatory management of the buffers around national parks and sanctuaries as well as the corridors linking them.

3. The report of the inter-State committee was considered by the Indian Board for Wild Life and its Standing Committee, which further recommended comprehensive amendments to the Wild Life Act, on the basis of the proposals of the said Committee.

4. A provision is proposed to be made in the Wild Life Act for creation of two new types of reserves, i.e., Conservation Reserves and Community Reserves. Conservation Reserve would be an area owned by the State Governments adjacent to national parks and sanctuaries for protecting the landscape, seascape and habitat of fauna and flora. Further, it is also proposed to empower the State Governments to notify any community land or private land as community reserve provided that the members of that community or individuals concerned are agreeable to offer such areas for protecting the fauna and flora, as well as their traditions, cultures and practices. The declaration of these two new types of reserves, i.e., conservation reserve and community reserve are aimed at improving the socio-economic conditions of the people living in those areas as well as conservation of wild

life. Conservation reserve and community reserve would be managed on the principles of sustainable utilisation of forest produce. The members of the local communities would be involved in their management through management committees.

For the better understanding of the wild life laws of the different countries only those provisions have been taken into consideration which are important and relevant to the subject of research. In order to make a systematic study of the wild life of the different countries taken for study in the first chapter I have divided them in 8 categories. As this chapter also deals with the laws (Indian) to protect the Wild Life hence in order to built up a proper comparison I have categorised the laws exactly in the same manner as adopted in Chapter 1.

Authorities

Section 2: Clause [10][(12A) "Forest Officer" means the Forest Officer appointed under clause (2) of section 2 of the Indian Forest Act, 1927;]

Section 3 to 8 : Deals with authorities to be appointed or constituted under the Act, Section 3 Appointment of Director and other officers:

(1) The Central Government May, for the purposes of this Act, appoint:

(a) A Director of Wild Life Preservation.

[11][* * *]

(c) Such other officers and employees as may be necessary.

(2) In the performance of his duties and exercise of his powers by or under this Act, the Director shall be subject to such general or special directions, as the Central Government may, from time to time, give.

[12][(3) The officers and other employees appointed under this section shall be required to assist the Director.]

Section 4 Appointment of Life Warden and other officers:

---

10. Ins. by Act 44 of 1991, Sec. 5 (w.e.f. 2-10-1991).
11. Cl. (b) ommitted by the Wild Life (Protection Amendment Act, 2002 S. 4(i).
12. Substituted by the Wild Life (Protection) Amendment Act, 2002, S. 4(ii), for sub-S. (3).

(1) The State Government may, for the purposes of this Act, appoint,—

(a) A Chief Wild Life Warden;
(b) Wild Life Wardens;[13][*]
[14][(bb) Honorary Wild Life Wardens;]
(c) Such other officers and employees as may be necessary.

(2) In the performance of his duties and exercise of his powers by or under this Act, the Chief Wild Life Warden shall be subject to such general or special directions, as the State Government may, from time to time, give.

(3) [15][The Wild Life Warden, the Honorary Wild Life Warden] and other officers and employees appointed under this section shall be subordinate to the Chief Wild Life Warden.

Section [16][5-A Constitution of the National Board for Wild Life.

Section 5-B Standing Committee of the National Board.

Section 5-C Functions of the National Board.]

Section [17][6 Constitution of State Board of Wild Life.]

Section 8 Duties of [18][State Board for Wild Life].—It shall be the duty of [18][State Board for Wild Life] to advise the State Government,—

[19][(a) in the selection and management of areas to be declared as protected areas.]
[20][(b) in formulation of the policy for protection and conservation of the wild life and specified plants;]

---

13. The word "and" omitted by Act 44 of 1991, S. 6 (w.e.f. 2-10-1991).
14. Substituted by the Wild Life (Protection) Amendment Act, 2002, S. 5 for Cl. (bb).]
15. Substituted by Act 44 of 1991, S. 6, for "The Wild Life Warden" (w.e.f. 2-10-1991).
16. Inserted by the Wild Life (Protection) Amendment Act, 2002, S. 6.
17. Substituted by the Wild Life (Protection) Amendment Act, 2002, S. 7, for S. 6.
18. Substituted by the Wild Life (Protection) Amendment Act, 2002 S. 8(i), for "the Wild Life Advisory Board").
19. Substituted by the Wild Life (Protection) Amendment Act, 2002 S. 8 (ii), for Cl.(a).
20. Substituted by Act 44 of 1991, S. 8 (w.e.f. 2-10-1991).

(c) In any matter relating to the amendment of any Schedule;[21][*]

[22][(cc) in relation to the measures to be taken for harmonising the needs of the tribals and other dwellers of the forest with the protection and conservation of wild life; and]

(d) in any other matter connected with the protection of wild life which may be referred to it by the State Government.

Section 9: Prohibition of hunting: No person shall hunt any wild animal specified in schedules I, II, III and IV except as provided under section 11 and section 12.

Ownership of the Wild Life

Section 2: Clause (14) "Government property" means any property referred to in section 39; [23][or section I7H;]

39. Wild animals, etc., to be Government property:

(1) Every—

(a) wild animal, other than vermin, which is hunted under section 11 or sub-section (1) of section 29 or subsection (6) of section 35 or kept or (bred in captivity or hunted) in contravention of any provision of this Act or any rule or order made thereunder or found dead, or killed by [24][***] mistake; and

(b) animal article, trophy or uncured trophy or meat derived from any wild animal referred to in clause (a) in respect of which any offence against this Act or any rule or order made thereunder has been committed;

[25][(c) ivory imported into India and an article made from such ivory in respect of which any offence against this Act or any rule or order made thereunder has been committed.

(d) vehicle, vessel, weapon, trap or tool that has been used for committing an offence and has been seized under the

21. The word "and" Omitted by Act 44 of 1991, sec. 8 (w.e.f. 2-10-1991).
22. Inserted by Act 44 of 1991, Sec. 8 (w.e.f. 2-10-1991).
23. Inserted by Act 44 of 1991, Sec. 5(w.e.f. 2-10-1991).
24. Substituted by Act 44 of 1991, S. 27, for "bred in captivity" (w.e.f. 2-10-1991).
25. Inserted by Act, 44 of 1991, S. 27 (w.e.f. 2-10-1991).

provisions of this Act,] shall be the property of the State Government, and, where such animal is hunted in a Sanctuary or National Park declared by the Central Government, such animal or any animal article, trophy, uncured trophy or meat [26][derived from such animal, or any vehicle, vessel, weapon, trap or tool used in such hunting] shall be the property of the Central Government.

(2) Any person who obtains, by any means, the possession of Government property, shall, within forty-eight hours from obtaining such possession, make a report as to the obtaining of such possession to the nearest police station or the authorised officer shall, if so required, hand over such property to the officer-in-charge of such police station or such authorised officer, as the case may be.

(3) No person shall, without the previous permission in writing of the Chief Wild Life Warden or the authorised officer—

(a) acquire or keep in his possession, custody or control, or
(b) transfer to any person, whether by way of gift, sale or otherwise, or
(c) destroy or damage, such Government property.

Categories of Protected Areas

Under this Act there are four categories of protected areas have been mentioned i.e. :

(1) National Parks
(2) Sanctuaries
(3) Conservation Reserve
(4) Community Reserve

Section 2 of the Act Defines

Clause [27][(24-A) "Protected area" means a National Park, a sanctuary, a conservation reserve or a community reserve notified under sections 18, 35, 36-A and 36-C of the Act;]

26. Substituted by Act 44 of 1991, S. 27, for "derived from such animal" (w.e.f. 2-10-1991).
27. Inserted by the Wild Life (Protection) Amendment Act, 2002, S.3(j).

Clause 21 "National Park" means an area declared, whether under section 35 or section 38, or deemed, under sub-section (3) of section 66, to be declared, as. a National Park;

Clause [[28][(25-B) "reserve forest" means the forest declared to be reserved by the State Government under section 20 of the Indian Forest Act, 1927 (16 of 1927), or declared as such under any other State Act;

Clause 26 "Sanctuary" means an area declared as a sanctuary by' notification under the provisions of Chapter IV of this Act and shall also include a deemed sanctuary under sub-section (4) of section 66;]

Declaration of Protected Areas for Wild Life

18. *Declaration of Sanctuary*: (1) The State Government may, by notification, declare its intention to constitute any area other than an area comprised within any reserve forest or the territorial waters as a sanctuary, if it considers that such area is of adequate ecological, fauna, floral, geomorphologic, natural or zoological significance, for the purpose of protecting, propagating or developing wild life or its environment.

(2) The notification referred to in sub-section (1) hall specify, as nearly as possible, the situation and limits of such area.

Explanation: for the purposes of this section it shall be sufficient to describe the area by roads, rivers, bridges or other well-known or readily intelligible boundaries.

26A. *Declaration of area as sanctuary*: (1) When—

(a) A notification has been issued under section 18 and the period for preferring claims has elapsed, and all claims, if any, made in relation to any land in an area intended to be declared as a sanctuary, have been disposed of by the State Government; or

(b) Any area comprised within any reserve forest or any part of the territorial waters, which is considered by the State Government to be of adequate ecological, fauna, floral, geomorphologic, natural or zoological

28. Substituted by the Wild Life (Protection) Amendment Act, 2002, S. 3(k), for Cls. (25-B) and (26).

significance for the purpose of protecting, propagating or developing wild life or its environment, is to be included in a sanctuary,

The State Government shall issue a notification specifying the limits of the area which shall be comprised within the sanctuary and declare that the said area shall be sanctuary on and from such date as may be specified in the notification:

Provided that where any part of the territorial waters is to be so included, prior concurrence of the Central Government shall be obtained by the State Government:

Provided further that the limits of the area of the territorial water to be included in the sanctuary shall be determined in consultation with the Chief Naval Hydrographic or the Central Government and after taking adequate measures to protect the occupational interest of the local fishermen.

(2) Notwithstanding any thing contained in sub-section 91, the right of innocent passage of any vessel or boat through the territorial waters shall not be affected by the notification issued under sub-section (1).

(3) No alteration of the boundaries of sanctuary shall be made except on a resolution passed by the legislature of the State.

35. *Declaration of National Parks* : (1) Wherever it appears to the State Government that an area, whether within a sanctuary or not, is, by reason of its ecological, fauna, floral, geomorphologic or zoological association or importance, needed to be constituted as a National Park for the purpose of protecting, propagating or developing wild life therein or its environment, it may, by notification, declare its intention to constitute such area as a National Park.

Provided that where any part of the territorial waters is proposed to be included in such National Park, the provisions of section 26A, shall as far as may be, apply in relation to the declaration of a National Park as they apply in relation to the declaration of a sanctuary.

(2) The notification referred to in sub-section (1) shall define the limits of the area, which is intended to be declared as a National Park.

(3) Where any area is intended to be declared as a National Park, the provisions of sections [19 to 26A (both inclusive except clause (c) of sub-section (2) of section 24)] shall, as far as may be, apply to the investigation and determination of claims, and extinguishments of rights, in relation to any land in such area as they apply to the said matters in relation to any land in a sanctuary.

(4) When the following events have occurred, namely:

(a) The period for preferring claims has elapsed, and all claims, if any, made in relation to any and in an area intended to be declared as a National Park, have been disposed of by the State Government and

(b) All rights in respect of lands proposed to be included in the National Park have become vested in the State Government, The State Government shall publish a notification specifying the limits of the area which shall be comprised within the National Park and declare that the said area shall be a National Park on and from such date as may be specified in the notification.

(5) No alteration of the boundaries of a National Park shall be made except on a resolution passed by the Legislature of the State.

(6) No person shall destroy, exploit or remove any wild life from a National Park or destroy or damage the habitat of any wild animal or deprive any wild animal of its habitat within such National Park except under and in accordance with a permit granted by the Chief Wild Life Warden and no such permit shall be granted unless the State Government, being satisfied that such destruction, exploitation or removal of wild life from the National Park is necessary for the improvement and better management of wild life therein, authorises the issue of such permit.

(7) No grazing of any (livestock) shall be permitted in a National Park and no (livestock) shall be allowed to enter therein except where such (livestock) is used as a vehicle by a person authorised to enter such National Park.

(8) The provisions of sections 27 and 28, sections 30 to 32 (both inclusive), and clauses (a), (b) and (c) of (section 33, section 33A) and section 34 shall, as far as may be, apply in relation to a National Park as they apply in relation to a sanctuary.

[29][36-A. *Declaration and Management of a Conservation Reserve*—(1) The State Government may, after having consultations with the local communities, declare any area owned by the Government, particularly the areas adjacent to National Parks and sanctuaries and those areas which link one protected are with another, as a Conservation Reserve for protecting landscapes, seascapes, flora and fauna and their habitat:

Provided that where the Conservation Reserve includes any land owned by the Central Government, its prior concurrence shall be obtained before making such declaration.

(2) The provisions of sub-section (2) of section 18, sub-sections (2), (3) and (4) of section 27, sections 30, 32 and clauses (b) and (c) of section 33 shall, as far as may be, apply in relation to a Conservation Reserve as they apply in relation to a sanctuary.

36-C *Declaration and Management of Community Reserve*—(1) The State Government may, where the community or an individual has volunteered to conserve wild life and its habitat, declare any private of community land not comprised within a National Park, sanctuary or a Conservation Reserve, as a Community Reserve, for protecting fauna, flora and traditional or cultural conservation values and practices.

(2) The provisions of sub-section (2) of section 18, sub-sections (2), (3) and (4) of section 27, sections 30, 32 and clauses (b) and (c) of section 33 shall, as far as may be, apply in relation to a Community Reserve as they apply in relation to a sanctuary.

(3) After the issue of notification under sub-section (1), no change in the land use pattern shall be made within the Community Reserve, except in accordance with a resolution passed by the Management Committee and approval of the same by the State Government.

---

29. Inserted by the Wild Life (Protection) Amendment Act, 2002, S. 20.

38. Power of Central Government to declare areas as sanctuaries or National Parks:

(1) Where the State Government leases or otherwise transfers any area under its control, not being an area within a sanctuary, to the Central Government, the Central Government may, if it is satisfied that the conditions specified in section 18 are fulfilled in relation to the area so transferred to it, declare such area, by notification, to be sanctuary and the provisions of (sections 18 to 35) (both inclusive), 54 and 55 shall apply in relation to such sanctuary as they apply in relation to a sanctuary declared by the State Government.

(2) The Central Government may, if it is satisfied that the conditions specified in section 35 are fulfilled in relation to any area referred to in sub-section (1), whether or not such area has been declared, to be a sanctuary by the Central Government or the State Government, declare such area, by notification, to be a National Park and the provisions of sections 35, 54 and 55 shall apply in relation to such National Park as they apply in relation to a National Park declared by the State Government.

(3) In relation to a sanctuary or National Park declared by the Central Government, the powers and duties of the Chief Wild Life Warden under the sections referred to in sub-sections (1) and (2), shall be exercised and discharged by the Director or by such other officer as may be authorised by the Director in this behalf and references, in the sections aforesaid, to the State Government shall be construed as reference to the Central Government and references therein to the Legislature of the State shall be construed as a reference to Parliament.

Procedure for Acquisition of Lands

Section 25: Acquisition Proceedings: (1) For the purpose of acquiring such land, or rights in or over such land:

(a) The Collector shall be deemed to be a Collector, proceeding under the Land Acquisition Act, 1894 (1 to 1894).

(b) The claimant shall be deemed to be a person interested and appearing before him in pursuance of a notice given under section 9 of that Act;

(c) The provisions of the sections, preceding section 9 of that Act, shall be deemed to have been complied with;

(d) Where the claimant does not accept the award made in his favour in the matter of compensation, he shall be deemed, within the meaning of section 18 of that Act, to be a person interested who has not accepted the award, and shall be entitled to proceed to claim relief against the award under the provisions of Part III of that Act;

(e) The Collector, with the consent of the claimant, or the Court, with the consent of both the parties, may award compensation in land or money or partly in land and partly in money; and

(f) In the case of the stoppage of a public way or a common pasture, the Collector may, with the previous sanction of the State Government, provide for an alternative public way or common pasture, as far as may be practicable or convenient.

(2) The acquisition under this Act of any land or interest therein shall be deemed to be acquisition for a public purpose.

[30][25-A. Time-limit for completion of acquisition proceedings—

(1) The collector shall, as far as possible, complete the proceedings under sections 19 to 25 (both inclusive), within a period of two years from the date of notification of declaration of sanctuary under section 18.

(2) The notification shall not lapse if, for any reasons, the proceedings are not completed within a period of two years.]

30. Inserted by the Wild Life (Protection) Amendment Act, 2002, S. 13.

Administrative Provisions

19. *Collector to Determine Rights:* [31][When a notification has been issued under section 18,] the Collector shall inquire into, and determine, the existence, nature and extent of the rights of any person in or over the land comprised within the limits of the sanctuary.

20. *Bar of Accrual of Rights*: After the issue of a notification under section 18, no right shall be acquired in, on or over the land comprised within the limits of the area specified in such notification, except by succession, testamentary or interstate.

21. *Proclamation by Collector* : When a notification has been issued under section 18, the Collector shall [32](within a period of sixty days,] publish in the regional language in every town and village in or in the neighbourhood of the area comprised therein, as proclamation—

(a) Specifying, as nearly as possible, the situation and the limits of the sanctuary; and
(b) Requiring any person, claiming any right mentioned in section 19, to prepare before the Collector, within two months from the date of such proclamation, a written claim in the prescribed from, specifying the nature and extent of such right with necessary details and the amount and particulars of compensation, if any, claimed in respect thereof.

22. *Inquiry by Collector*: The Collector shall, after service of the prescribed notice upon the claimant, expeditiously inquire into—

(a) The claim preferred before him under clause (b) of section 21, and
(b) The existence of any right mentioned in section 19 and not claimed under clause (b) of section 21.

So far as the same may be ascertainable from the records of the State Government and the evidence of any person acquainted with the same.

---

31. Substituted by Act 44 of 1991, S. 16.
32. Inserted by the Wild Life (Protection) Amendment Act, 2002, S. 12.

23. *Powers of Collector*: For the purpose of such inquiry, the Collector may exercise the following powers, namely:

(a) The power to enter minor upon any land and to survey, demarcate and make a map of the same or to authorise any other officer to do so;
(b) The same powers as are vested in a civil court for the trial of suits.

27. Restriction on entry in sanctuary: (1) Person other than,—

(a) A public servant on duty,
(b) A person who has been permitted by the Chief Wild, Life Warden or the authorised officer to reside within the limits of the sanctuary.
(c) A person who has any right over immovable property within the limits of the sanctuary.
(d) A person passing through the sanctuary along a public highway, an
(e) The dependant of the person referred to in clause (a), clause (b) or clause (c), shall enter or reside in the sanctuary, except under and in accordance with the conditions of a permit granted under section 28.

(2) Every person shall, so long as he resides in the sanctuary, be bound—

(a) To prevent the commission, in the sanctuary, of an offence against this Act;
(b) Where there is reason to believe that any such offence against this Act has been committed in such sanctuary, to help in discovering and arresting the offender;
(c) To report the death of any wild animal and to safeguard its remains until the Chief Wild Life Warden or the authorised officer takes charge thereof;
(d) To extinguish any fire in such sanctuary of which he has knowledge or information and to prevent from spreading, by any lawful means in his poor, any fire-

within the vicinity of such sanctuary of which he has knowledge or information; and

(e) To assistant Forest Officer, Chief Wild Life Warden, Wild Life Warden or Police Officer demanding his aid for preventing the commission of any offence against this Act or in the investigation of any such offence.

(3) No person shall, with intent to cause damage to any boundary-mark of a sanctuary or to cause wrongful gain as defined in the Indian Penal Code (45 of 1860), alter, destroy, move or deface such boundary-mark.

(4) No person shall tease or molest any wild animal or litter the grounds of sanctuary.

28. *Grant of Permit* : (1) The Chief Wild Life Warden, may, on application, grant to any person a permit to enter or reside in a sanctuary for all or any of the following purposes, namely:

(a) investigation or study of wild life and purposes ancillary or incidental thereto;
(b) photography;
(c) scientific research;
(d) tourism;
(e) transaction of lawful business with any person residing in the sanctuary.

(2) A permit to enter or reside in a sanctuary shall be issued subject to such conditions and on payment of such fee as may be prescribed.

[33][29. Destruction, etc. in a sanctuary prohibited without a permit:

No person shall destroy, exploit or remove any wild life including forest produce from a sanctuary or destroy or damage or divert the habitat of any wild animal by any act whatsoever or divert, stop or enhance the flow of water into or outside the sanctuary, except under and in accordance with a permit granted by the Chief Wild Life Warden, and

33. Substituted by the Wild Life (Protection) Amendment Act, 2002, S. 15, for S. 29.

no such permit shall be granted unless the State Government being satisfied in consultation with the Board that such removal of wild life from the sanctuary or the change in flow of water into or outside the sanctuary is necessary for the improvement and better management of wild life therein, authorises the issue of such permit.

Provide that where the forest produce is removed from a sanctuary the same may be used for meeting the personal bonafide needs of the people living in and around the sanctuary and shall not be used for any commercial purpose.

Explanation—For the purposes of this section, grazing or movement of livestock permitted under clause(d) of section 33 shall not be deemed to be an act prohibited under this section.

30. *Causing Fire Prohibited*: No person shall set fire to a sanctuary, or kindle any fire, or leave any fire burning, in a sanctuary, in such manner as to endanger such sanctuary.

31. *Prohibition of Entry into Sanctuary with Weapon*: No person shall enter a sanctuary with any weapon except with the previous permission in writing of the Chief Wild Life Warden or the authorised officer.

32. *Ban on use of Injurious Substances*: No person shall use in a sanctuary, chemicals, explosives, or any other substances, which may cause injury to or endanger, any wild life in such sanctuary.

33. *Control of Sanctuaries*: The Chief Wild Life Warden shall be the authority who shall control, manage and maintain all sanctuaries and for that purpose, within the limits of any sanctuary—

(a) may construct such roads, bridges, buildings, fences or barrier gates, and carry out such other works as he may consider necessary for the purposes of such sanctuary : [34][Provided that no construction of commercial tourist lodges, hotels, zoos and safari parks shall be undertaken inside a sanctuary except with the prior approval of the National Board;]

34. Inserted by the Wild Life (protection) Amendment Act, 2002, S.16.

(b) shall take such steps as will ensure the security of wild animals in the sanctuary and the preservation of the sanctuary and wild animals therein;

(c) may take such measures, in the interests of wild life, a he may consider necessary for the improvement of any habitat;

(d) may regulate, control or prohibit, in keeping with the interests of wild life, the grazing or movement of [35][livestock.]

34. *Registration of certain persons in possession of arms*: (1) Within three months from the declaration of any area as a sanctuary, every person residing in or within ten kilometres of any such sanctuary and holding a licence granted under the Arms Act, 1959 (54 of 1959), for the possession of arms or exempted from the provisions of that Act and possessing arms, shall apply in such form, on payment of such fee and within such time as may be prescribed, to the Chief Wild Life Warden or the authorised officer, for the registration of his name.

[36][34-A. *Power to remove encroachment*—(1) Notwithstanding anything contained in any other law for the time being in force, any officer not below the rank of any officer not below the rank of an Assistant Conservator of Forests may,—

(a) evict any person from a sanctuary or National Park, who unauthorisedly occupies Government land in contravention of the provisions of this Act;

(b) remove any unauthorised structures, buildings, or constructions erected on any Government land within any sanctuary or National Park and all the things, tools and effects belonging to such persons shall be confiscated, by an order of an officer not below the rank of the Deputy Conservator of Forests:

Provided that no such order shall be passed unless the affected persons is given an opportunity of being heard.

---

35. Substituted by Act 44 of 1991, S. 21 for "Cattle", (w.e.f 2-10-1991).
36. Inserted by the Wild Life (Protection) Amendment Act, 2002, S.18.

(2) The provisions of this section shall apply notwithstanding any other penalty which may be inflicted for violation of any other provision of this Act].

[37][36-B *Conservation Reserve Management Committee*—(1) The State Government shall constitute a Conservation Reserve Management Committee to advise the Chief Wild Life Warden to conserve, manage and maintain the Conservation Reserve.

(2) The Committee shall consist of a representative of the forest or Wild Life Department, who shall be the Member Secretary of the Committee, on representative of each Village Panchayat in whose jurisdiction the reserve is located, three representatives of non-governmental organisations working in the field of wild life conservation and one representative each from the Department of Agriculture and Animal Husbandry.

(3) The Committee shall regulate its own procedure including the quorum.

36-D. *Community Reserve Management Committee*—(1) The State Government shall constitute a Community Reserve Management Committee, which shall be the authority responsible for conserving, maintaining and managing the Community Reserve.

(2) The Committee shall consist of five representatives nominated by the Village Panchayat or where such Panchayat does not exist by the member of the Gram Sabha and one representative of the State Forests or Wild Life Department under whose jurisdiction the Community Reserve is located.

(3) The Committee shall be the competent authority to prepare and implement the management plan for the Community Reserve and to take steps to ensure the protection of wild life and its habitat in the reserve.

(4) The Committee shall elect a Chairman who shall also the Honorary Wild Life Warden on the Community Reserve.

(5) The Committee shall regulate its own procedure including the quorum.

Penal Provisions

51. Penalties: (1) Any person who [38][contravenes any

37. Inserted by the Wild Life (Protection) Amendment Act, 2002, S. 20.
38. Substituted by Act 28 of 1986, S. 4, for "contravenes any provision of this Act" (w.e.f. 25-11-1986).

provision of this Act [39][(except Chapter VA] and section 38-1)] or any rule or order made thereunder or who commits a breach of any of the conditions of any licence or permit granted under this Act, shall be guilty of an offence against this Act, and shall, on conviction, be punishable with imprisonment for a term which may extend to [40][three years] or with fine which may extend to [40][twenty-five thousand rupees] or with both:

[41][Provided that where the offence committed is in relation to any animal specified in Schedule I or Part II of Schedule II or meat of any such animal or animal article, trophy or uncured trophy derived from such animal or where the offence relates to hunting in a sanctuary or a National Park or altering the boundaries of a sanctuary or a National Park, such offence shall be punishable with imprisonment for a term which shall not be less than three years but may extend to seven years and also with fine which shall not be less than ten thousand rupees.

Provided further that in the case of a second or subsequent offence of the nature mentioned in this sub-section, the term of imprisonment shall not be less than three years but may extend to seven years and also with fine which shall not be less than twenty-five thousand rupees.]

[42][(1A) Any person who contravenes any provisions of Chapter VA, shall be punishable with imprisonment for a term which shall not be less than [43][three years] but which may extend to seven years and also with fine which shall not be less than [43][ten thousand rupees].

[44][(1B) Any person who contravenes the provisions of section 38J, shall be punishable with imprisonment for a term

39. Substituted by Act 44 of 1991, S. 37, for "(except Chapter V-A)" (w.e.f. 2-10-1991).
40. Substituted by Act 44 of 1991, S. 37, for "two rupees" and "two thousand rupees". respectively (w.e.f. 2-10-1991).
41. Substituted by the Wild Life (Protection) Amendment Act, 2002, S. 30(i), for the first and second provisions.
42. Inserted by Act 28 of 1986, S.4 (w.e.f. 25-11-1986).
43. Substituted by the Wild Life (Protection) Amendment Act, 2002, S. 30(ii), for "one year" and "five thousand rupees", respectively.
44. Inserted by Act 44 of 1991, S. 37 (w.e.f. 2-10-1991).

which may extend to six months, or with fine which may extend to two thousand rupees, or with both:

Provided that in the case of a second or subsequent offence, the term of imprisonment may extend to one year, or with fine which may extend to five thousand rupees.]

(2) When any person is convicted of an offence against this Act, the Court trying the offence may order that any captive animal, wild animal, animal article, trophy [45][uncured trophy, meat, ivory imported into India or an article made from such ivory, any specified plant, or part or derivative thereof], in respect of which the offence has been committed, and any trap, tool, vehicle, vessel or weapon, used in the commission of the said offence be forfeited to the State Government and that any licence or permit, held by such person under the provisions of this Act, be cancelled.

(3) Such cancellation of licence or permit or such forfeiture shall be in addition to any other punishment that may be awarded for such offence.

(4) Where any person is convicted of an offence against this Act, the Court may direct that the licence, if any, granted to such person under the Arms Act, 1959 (54 of 1959), for possession of any arm with which an offence against this Act has been committed, shall be cancelled and that such person shall not be eligible for a licence under the Arms Act, 1959 (54 of 1959), for a period of five years from the date of conviction.

[46][(5) Nothing contained in section 360 of the Code of Criminal Procedure, 1973 (2 of 1974) or in the Probation of Offenders Act, 1958 (20 of 1958) shall apply to a person convicted of an offence with respect to hunting in a sanctuary or a national part or of an offence against any provision of Chapter VA unless such person is under eighteen years of age.]

[47][51-A Certain conditions to apply while granting bail- When any person accused of, the commission of any offence relating to Schedule I or Part National Park or wild life sanctuary or altering the boundaries of such parks and sanctuaries, is arrested under the provisions of the Act, then (2 of 1974) no such

45. Substituted by Act 44 of 1991, S. 37, for "uncured trophy or meal" (w.e.f. 2-10-1991).
46. Inserted by Act 44 of 1991, S. 37 (w.e.f. 2-10-1991).
47. Inserted by the Wild Life (Protection) Amendment Act, 2002, S. 31.

person who had been previously convicted of an offence under this Act shall, be released on bail unless—

(a) the Public Prosecutor has been given opportunity of opposing the release on bail; and (b) where the Public Prosecutor opposes the application, the Court is satisfied that three are reasonable grounds for believing that he is not guilty of such offence and that he is not likely to commit any offence while on bail.]

52. Attempts and Abetment: Whoever attempts to contravene, or abets the contravention of, any of the provisions of this Act or of any rules or order made thereunder shall be deemed to have contravened that provision or rule or order, as the case may be.

53. Punishment for wrongful seizure: If any person, exercising powers under this Act, vexatiously and unnecessarily seizes the property of any other person on the pretence of seizing it for the reasons mentioned in section 50, he shall, on conviction, be punishable with imprisonment of a term which may extend to six months, or with fine which may extend to five hundred rupees, or with both.

[48][54. Power to compound offences: (1) (The Central Government may, by notification, empower the Director of Wild Life Preservation or any other officer not below the rank of Assistant Director of Wild Life Preservation and in the case of a State Government in the similar manner, empower the Chief Wild Life Warden or any officer of a rank not below the rank of a Deputy Conservator of Forests, to accept from any person against whom a reasonable suspicion exists that he has committed an offence against this Act, payment of a sum of money by way of composition of the offence which such person is suspected to have committed.

(a) to accept, from any person against who a reasonable suspicion exists that he has committed an offence against this Act, payment of a sum of money by way of composition of the offence which such person is suspected to have committed; and

48. Substituted by the Wild Life (Protection) Amendment Act, 2002, S. 32, for S. 54.

(b) when any property has been seized is liable to be forfeited, to release the same on payment of the value thereof as estimated by such officer.

(2) On payment of such sum of money or such value, or both, as the case may be, to such officer, the suspected person, if in custody, shall be discharged, and the property, other than Government property, if any, seized, shall be released and no further proceedings in respect of the offence shall be taken against such person.

(3) The officer compounding any offence may order the cancellation of any licence or permit granted under this Act to the offender, or if not empowered to do so, may approach an officer so empowered, for the cancellation of such licence or permit.

(4) The sum of money accepted or agreed to be accepted as composition under clause (b) of sub-section (91) shall, in no case, exceed the sum of two thousand rupees:

Provided that no offence, for which a minimum period of imprisonment has been prescribed in sub-section (1) of section 51, shall be compounded]

[49][55. *Cognizance of Offences*: No Court shall take cognizance of any offence against this Act except on the complaint of any person other than—

(a) the Director of Wild Life Preservation or any other officer authorized in this behalf by the Central Government; or

[50][(aa) Member-Secretary, Central Zoo Authority in matters relating to violation of the provisions of Chapter IV-A or]

(b) the Chief Wild Life Warden, or any other officer authorised in this behalf by the State Government; [51][subject to such conditions as may be specified by that Government]; or

[52][(bb) the officer-in-charge of the zoo in respect of violation of provisions of section 38-j; or]

49. Substituted by Act 44 of 1991, S. 40, for S. 55 (w.e.f. 2-10-1991).
50. Inserted by the Wild Life (Protection) Amendment Act, 2002, S. 33(i).
51. Inserted by the Wild Life (Protection) Amendment Act, 2002, S. 33(ii).
52. Inserted by the Wild Life (Protection) Amendment Act, 2002, S. 33(iii).

(c) any person who has given notice of not less than sixty days, in the manner prescribed, of the alleged offence and of his intention to make a complaint to the Central Government or the State Government or the officer authorised as aforesaid.]

56. *Operation of other laws not barred*: Nothing in this Act shall be deemed to prevent any person from being prosecuted under any other law for the time being in force, for any act or omission which constitutes an offence against this act or from being liable under such other law to any higher punishment or penalty than that provided by this Act:

Provided that no person shall be punished twice for the same offence.

57. *Presumption to be made in certain cases*: Where, in any prosecution for an offence against this Act, it is established that a person is in possession, custody or control of any captive animal, animal article, meat (trophy, uncured trophy, specified plant, or part or derivative thereof) it shall be presumed until the contrary is proved, the burden of proving which shall lie on the accused, that such person is in unlawful possession, custody or control of such captive animal, animal article, meat (trophy, uncured trophy, specified plant, or part or derivative thereof).

58. *Offences by Companies*: (1) Where an offence against this Act has been committed by a company, every person who, at the time the offence was committed, was in charge of, and was responsible to, the company for the conduct of the business of the company as well as the company, shall be deemed to be guilty of the offence and shall be liable to be proceeded against and punished accordingly:

Provided that nothing contained in this sub-section shall render any such person liable to any punishment, if he proves that the offence was committed without his knowledge or that he exercised all due diligence to prevent the commission of such offence.

(2) Notwithstanding anything contained in sub-section (1), where an offence against this Act has been committed by a

company and it is proved that the offence has been committed with the consent or connivance of, or is attributable to any neglect on the part of, any director, manager, secretary or other officer of the company, such director, manager, secretary or other officer shall also be deemed to be guilty of that offence and shall be liable to be proceeded against and punished accordingly.

Explanation—For the purpose of this section,—

(a) "company" means any body corporate and includes a firm or other association of individuals; and

(b) "director", in relation to a firm, means a partner in the firm.

Settlement of the Tribal Rights

24. *Acquisition of Rights*: (1) In the case of a claim to a right in or over any land referred to in section 19, the Collector shall pass an order admitting or rejecting the same in whole or in part.

(2) If such claim is admitted in whole or in part, the Collector may either:

(a) Exclude such land from the limits of the proposed sanctuary, or

(b) Proceed to acquire such land or rights, except where by an agreement between the owner of such and or holder or rights and the Government, the owner or holder of such rights has agreed to surrender his rights to the Government, in or over such land, and on payment of such compensation, as is provided in the Land Acquisition Act, 1894 (1 to 1894).

(c) Allow, in consultation with the Chief Wild Life Warden, the continuance of any right of any person in or over any land within the limits of the sanctuary.

35. *Declaration of National Parks*—[53][*Explanation*—For the purpose of this section, in case of an area, whether within a sanctuary or not, where the rights have been extinguished and the land has become vested in the State Government under any Act or otherwise, such area may be notified by it, by a notification,

53. Inserted by the Wild Life (Protection) Amendment Act, 2002, S. 19(ii).

as a National Park and the proceedings under sections 19 to 26 (both inclusive, and the provisions of sub-sections (3) and (4) of this section shall not apply.]

65. *Right of Scheduled Tribes to be Protected*: Nothing in this Act shall affect the hunting rights conferred on the Schedule Tribes of the Nicobar Islands in the Union Territory of Andaman and Nicobar Islands by notification of the Andaman and Nicobar Territory of Andaman and Nicobar Islands by notification of the Andaman and Nicobar Administration, No. 40/67/F. No. G 635, Vol. III, dated the 28th April, 1967, published at pages 1 to 5 of the Extraordinary issue of the Andaman and Nicobar Gazette, dated the 28th April, 1967.

The Wild Life (Transactions and Taxidermy) Rules, 1973

These Rules were made by the Central Government, in exercise of the powers conferred by clause (b) of sub-section (1) of section 63 of the Wild Life (Protection) Act, 1972 (53 of 1972).

These rules extend to the whole of the States of Bihar, Gujarat, Haryana, Himachal Pradesh, Madhya Pradesh, and Uttar Pradesh.

Rule 2(e) States: "Specified animal" means any animal which is specified in schedule I; or part II of schedule II, to the Wild Life Protection Act and when is captured or kept or bred in captivity or found wild in nature."

No licensee shall :

(i) Acquire, receive, keep in his Control, custody, or possession, any specified animal or any animal article, trophy uncured trophy or meat derived there from or

(ii) Put under process of taxidermy or make animal article containing part or whole of such animal, except with the previous permission of the chief wild life warden or officer appointed by the State Government.

Format for Application form is prescribed in the Act.

On receipt of an application made under sub rule (2), the officer may, after making such inquiry he may think fit and within a period of fifteen days from the date of receipt of the application, either grant or refuse to grant the permission.

Provided that no such permission shall be granted unless the officer in satisfied that specified animal etc. has been lawfully acquired.

Where the officer refuses to grant the permission, he shall record the reasons. (Rule 3)

If permission granted, report regarding the stocks of such to the officer, after receiving such report officer, may arrange to affix identification marks, on such stock (Rule 4).

Rule 5: Prohibit the sale of such stocks, except to a person authorised to purchase by a permission granted by the officer and where the sale is affected the purchaser shall surrender the permission to the licensed dealer.

After receipt of Application for permission of purchase, officer may, within a period of ten days from the date of receipt of the application, either grant or refuse to grant the permission.

Every licensed dealer shall, at the time of each sale, issue a voucher in relation to the specified animal or animal article, trophy, referred to sub-rule (1), to the person authorized to purchase.

Every Licensed taxidermist or licensed manufacturer shall, at the time of returning the trophy or animal article, issue a voucher to the owner of the said trophy or animal article (Rule 6).

Rule 8 deals with Transport of specified animal etc. No licensee shall transport from one place to another within the State any specified animal etc., except with the previous permission of the officer.

Rule 9 deals with appeal any licensee or a person aggrieved by an order made by the Chief Wild Life Warden or any other officer granting the permission may prefer an appeal :

(i) if the order is made by an officer other than the chief wild life warden, to the Chief Wild Life Warden.

(ii) if the order is made by the Chief Wild Life Warden to the State Government.

In the case of an order passed in appeal by the Chief Wild Life Warden under clause (1) of sub-rule (1), a second appeal shall lie to the State Government.

The Wild Life (Stock Declaration) Central Rules, 1973

In exercise of the power conferred by clause (a) of sub-section (91) of section 63 of WLPA, 1972, the Central Government hereby makes the following rules:

They shall come into force in the State of Madhya Pradesh on the 25th Jan., 1973 and is other States and territories as central government may, by Notification appoint.

Rule 2 says that every manufacturer of or dealer in animal article or every dealer in captive animal, trophies, or uncured trophies or every taxidermist shall, within fifteen day from the commencement of the Wild Life (Protection) Act, 1972, declare his stock of animal articles, captive animals trophies, and uncured trophies, as the case may be as on the date of such declaration to the chief wild life warden in the form given.

The Wild Life (Protection) Licensing (Additional matter for Consideration) Rule, 1983

These rule made in the exercise of Clause (b) of section (4) of Section 44 of the WLPA, 1972.

They shall extend to whole of India except J & K.

Rule 3 : for the purpose of granting a license referred to in sub section (1) of section 44 of the WLPA, the Chief Wild Life Warden or the authorized officer, as the case may be, shall in addition to the matters specified in clause (b) of sub-section 4 of section 44, have regard there matters also:

(i) Capacity of the applicant to handle the business concerned within reference to facilities equipment and suitability of the primers for such business.

(ii) The source and the manner which the supplies for the business concerned would be obtained;

(iii) Member of license for the relevant business already in existence in the area concerned;

(iv) Implication, which the grant of such license would have on the hunting or trade of the wild animals concerned.

No such license shall be granted of the said implication relate to any wild animal specified in schedule I or part II of

Schedule II to the Act, except with the previous consultation of the Central Government.

The Wild Life (Protection) Rules, 1995

In exercise of power conferred by clause (K) of sub- section (1) of section 63 of the Wild Life (Protection) Act, 1972. Central Government makes these rules.

Rule 3 was Provided the Manner of the Notice

The notice to the Central or the State Government or any authorised officer, as the case may be, shall be given in form prescribed in the rules.

Notice also send by registered post to:

(a) The Director of Wild Life Protection, Govt. of India in the Ministry of Environment and Forest, New Delhi.

(b) (i) The Secretary to the concerned State Govt. Union Territory in charge of Wild Life.

(ii) The Chief Wild Life Warden of the concerned State Government or Union Territory.

(iv) Any authorised officer of State Govt./U.T.

The Wild Life (Specified Plants—Conditions for Possession by Licensee) Rules, 1995

In exercise of power conferred by clause (a) of sub-section (1) of section 63 of Wild Life (Protection) Act, 1972, the Central Government makes the rules.

These rules came in the forced from 2.10.1991.

Rule 3: (1) No licensee shall acquire or receive or keep in his control, custody or possession any specified plant or part or derivative there of in respect of which a declaration under section 17E of Act has not been made.

(2) No licensee shall acquire, purchase or receive any specified plant or part or derivative there of from any person other than a licensed dealer in specified plants or a cultivator having a license for cultivation of specified plants under the Act.

(3) Licensee shall keep the stock of specified plants so purchased by him only in the premises approved by the Chief Wild Life warden of the State.

The Recognition of Zoo Rules, 1992

On 4th August 1992 it published in the Gazette of India, in exercise of the power conferred by clause (f) and (g) of sub-section (91) of section 63 of the Wild Life (Protection) Act, 1972.

Under Rûle 2 Sub-rule (b) "Enclosure" means any accommodation provided for zoo animals.

These Rules describe the recognition of zoo, the Application form fees. Authorities, Renewal of Recognition. Rule of Classified the Zoos. For the purpose of deciding standards and norms for recognition. Zoos shall be classified in to four categories Large, Medium, small and mini on the basis the area, No. of animal and their variety exhibited.

Rule 10: deals Standards and norms subject to which recognition under section 38H of the WLPA shall be granted, like general, administrative and staffing pattern animal Enclosures—Deposing, Dimensions and other Essential Features, Hygiene Feeding and Upkeep, Animal Care, Health and Treatment, veterinary facilities, Breeding of animals, maintenance of Records and Submission of inventory to the Central Zoo authority, education and Research, visitor faculties, development and planning.

National Zoo Policy, 1998

The preamble of the policy says that the growing awareness for nature and wild life conservation made zoos a popular institution. Estimate indicates that 10% of the world's population visits zoos every year. There are about 350 animal collections in India, which are visited by more than 50 million people annually.

The need for making conservation as one of the main objectives of Management of zoos was realised by Government of India soon after Independence and the Indian Board for committee on Management of zoo in X/OV 1972 and its recommendation were accepted in June 1973. The recommendations are relevant even now for improving the management of zoos.

The National Wild Life Action Plan, 1972 again emphasis the role of exist conservation in national conservation efforts. However, because of varied ownership patterns and divergent nature of animal collections not much was achieved.

The main emphasis was given to educational, scientific and conservational aspects of zoos.

The National zoo policy aims at given proper direction and thrust to the management of zoos by mustering cooperation and participation of all concerned.

The main objective of the zoos shall be to complement and strengthen the national efforts in conservation of the rich biodiversity of the country, particularly the wild fauna.

For achieving these objective some strategy are proposed. Like Rural Policy about zoos, Acquisition of animals, housing or health care of animals for upkeep of animal collection proper diet and water, health care, research and Training on biological, behaviour, nutrition and veterinary aspects of animals, educational activity, etc.

The Forest (Conservation) Act, 1980[4]

An Act to provide for the conservation of forests and for matters connected herewith on ancillary or incidental thereto.

It came in to force from 25th Oct., 1980 and extends to the whole of India except J&K.

According to section 2, Notwithstanding any thing contained in any other law for the time being in force in a state, no state Government or other authority shall make, except with the prior approval of the Central Government, any order directing :

(i) That any reserved forest or any portion thereof, shall case to be reserved.

(ii) That any forest land or any portion there of may be used for any non-forest purpose.

(iii) That any forest land or any portion there of may be assigned by way of lease or otherwise to any private person or to any authority; corporation, agency or any other organisation not owned managed or controlled by Government.

(iv) That any forest land or any portion there of may be caused of threes which have grown naturally in that land or position for the purpose of using it for afforest ration.

By the Act 69 of 1988, section 2 this explanation was substituted:

For the purposes of this section "non forest purpose" means the breaking-up of cleaning or any forest and or portion thereof for—

(a) The cultivation of tea, coffee, spices, rubber, palms, oil-bearing plants, horticulture crops or medicinal plants,
(b) Any purpose other than afforestation.

But does not include any work relating or ancillary to conservation, development and management of forests and wild-life, namely the establishment of check-posts, fire lines, wireless communications and construction of fencing, bridges and culverts, dams, water holes, trench marks, boundary marks, pipelines or other like purposes.

Section 3 has provision for constitution of Advisory Committee section 3A and 3B inserted by Act 69 of 1988, section 3, w.e.f. 15.3.1989.

According to set 3A wherever contravenes or abets the contravention of any of the provisions of section 2, shall be punishable with simple imprisonment for a period, which may extend to fifteen days.

Set 3B deals with offences by authorities and Government Departments. Under this act has been when any offence a committed.

(a) By any department of government, the head of the department, or
(b) By any authority, every person who, at the time the offence was committed, was directly in charge of and was responsible to, the authority for the conduct of the business the authors as well as the authority.

Shall be deemed to be guilty of the offence and shall be liable to be proceeded against and punished accordingly.

Section 4. Give power to Central Government to make rules.

In exercise of that power the Central Govt. made rule, these rules known as forest (conservation) Rules, 1981.

Rules have provision for a committee (2A) and conduct of business of the committee (set˙3).

Section 4 deals with procedure to make proposal by State Government or other authority:

(1) Every State Govt. or other authority seeking the prior approval under section 2 shall send its proposal to the Central Government in the form appended to these rules.

Provided that all proposals involving clearing of naturally grown trees in forest land or portion there of for the purpose of using it for re-afforestation shall be sent in the form of working plan/management plan.

Every proposal shall be sent to secretary to the Govt. of India.

Provided that all proposal of involving forest land upto twenty hectares and proposals involving cleaning of naturally grown trees in forest land or portion thereof for the purpose of using it for re-afforestation shall be sent to the Chief Conservator of forests/conservation of forests of the consented region office of the ministry of Environment and forest.

Section 5: The Central Govt. shall refer every proposal received by it under sub rule (1) of rule, 4 to the committee for its advice thereon if the area of the forestland involved is more than twenty hectares.

The Central Govt. shall, after considering the advice of the committee tendered under rule 5 and after such further enquiry as it may consider necessary grant approval to the proposal with or without conditions or reject the same.

After the discussion of the Wild Life Acts of the different countries like: Japan, Canada, China, Malawi and Bulgaria in Chapter 1 and the various Indian laws to protect the wild life like: Indian forest Act, Constitutional provisions for the protect of Wild Life, Cattle Trespass Act, Indian Wild Life Act and different rules made under the Wild Life Protection Act in Chapter 2.

I feet that mere discussion of the laws is not sufficient as the study of the laws will be incomplete without proper comparisons and observation. Hence the necessity to compare and observe the wild life laws of the different countries with that of India in order to reach a proper conclusion which will be under the heading observations.

OBSERVATIONS

(1) Authority

After studying the provisions relating to authorities in the different countries I found that the administration of the protected areas is given to various authorities. The authorities are known by various names as Park Directorates and Regional Inspectorates of Environment and Waters in Bulgaria, Prefectural Governor in Japan, Chief Park and Wild Life Officer and Honorary Parks and Wild Life Officer in Malawi, with other subordinate officers who shall be responsible for the administration subject to any general or special direction of the Minister. When I compared these with China I observed that no such provisions specifically mention the name of the authority for administration. Instead a mention has been made that the Department of Forestry and Fishery administration under the State Council shall be respectively responsible for the nationwide administration of terrestrial and aquatic wild life. In Canada the authority is distinguished as Wild Life Officers.

As compared with the Indian Wild Life (Protection) Act, the study reveals that Section 2: Clause (12A) and Sections 3 to 8 deal with the authorities. They are known by the names: Director of Wild Life Preservation, Chief Wild Life Warden, Wild Life Warden, Hon. Wild Life Warden alongwith other subordinate officers.

(2) Ownership

In Bulgaria, Parks are exclusive property of the State that include plant and animal species, whereas in Canada ownership of wild life is not specifically mentioned instead the term "Public Land" has been used which means land belonging to her Majesty. In China, ownership of the wild life goes to the State as mentioned in Article 3. In Japan, I have not come across any such provision, which declare ownership of the wild life there. In Malawi it is stated in Section 4 of Part I that complete land, which pertains to wild animals and plants, is vested in possession of the President.

In India the right of ownership of land for the wild life is vested in the hands of the sovereign, which is the State. Section 39 of the Wild Life Act declares, wild animals, etc., to be the property of the government. Thus it can be observed that out of six countries only one i.e. Japan has not mentioned clearly the ownership of the wild life there.

(3) Categories of Protected Areas

In Bulgaria there are six categories of protected areas namely: Strict Nature Reserve, National Park, Natural Monument, Menaged Reserve, Natural Park and Protected Site. In Canada no specific mention of the protected areas is made, on the contrary the procedure for the protection of wild life has been given.

In China as far as I understand three categories of protected areas have been given: nature reserves, areas closed to hunting and areas close to hunting during seasons. The activities which are harmful to the living and breeding of wild life shall be prohibited in these areas.

Japan also have 3 categories of protected areas, like, sanctuary, special sanctuary, and temporary hunting prohibited area.

In India this aspect is dealt in different sections of the Wild Life (Protection) Act, 1972. Section 2 Clause 24A inserted by Wild Life (Protection) Amendment Act, 2002 defines Protected Areas as:

(1) National Park (Clause 21 of Section 2, Section 35 or Section 38).
(2) Sanctuary (Clause 26 of Section 2, Section 18, Section 26A, Subsection 4 of Section 66).
(3) Conservation Reserve (36-A).
(4) Community Reserve (36-C).

There is another aspect which has been observed during my study which need mention, i.e., "reserve forest" (the forest declared to be reserved by the State Government under section 20 of the Indian Forest Act, 1927). Hence it can be observed that except Canada all other countries taken for study have specifically mentioned the category of the protected areas.

(4) Declaration of Protected Areas

After examining the provisions relating to the declaration of the protected areas in different countries taken for study I could construe that different procedures have been adopted for the declarations. In Bulgaria the declaration and changes within the protected areas are made by the Minister of Environment and Waters. Articles 36-40 deal with the procedure whereas in Canada no such procedure has been laid down in Canada Wild Life Act (1985). In China no direct reference to the procedure regarding declaration of protected areas is given but it has been mentioned in Article 7 that the departments of forestry and fishery administration under the State Council shall be respectively responsible for the nationwide administration of terrestrial and aquatic wild life. When compared with Japan it was found that in Article 8-2 the Director-General and the Prefectural Governor has power to establish protected areas in accordance with the cabinet order.

In Malawi the power of declaration of the protected areas is vested in the Minister. The procedure of declaration has been outlined in Article 26(1) and 28(i).

(5) Procedure of Acquisition of Land

Except China, in all the other countries procedure of acquisition of land has been specifically mentioned. In Bulgaria the acquisition takes place in consonance with the provisions laid down under the State Property Act. In Canada the power lies with the Governor in Council who may authorise the Minister for the acquisition of land. The procedure of acquisition is not clearly mentioned in the Wild Life Protection Act and Hunting laws and Related Legislation (1918) of Japan but a provision to compensate the loss is given in Article 8-2. In Malawi it has been observed that the procedure for the acquisition of land is made in accordance with the provisions of the Land Act and Land Acquisition Act.

In India acquisition of rights are discussed in Section 25 and acquisition proceedings are mentioned in Section 25-A of the Wild Life (Protection) Act, 1972.

(6) Administrative Provisions

Chapter six of Protected Areas Law, 1998 of Bulgaria deals with administrative and penal provisions. This chapter is divided into two Sections in which Section 1 deals with the Compulsory Administrative Measures which spread from Article

78 to 80. Article 78 talks of the administrative violations and their harmful consequences Article 80 provides procedure for the appeal against the administrative measures.

In Canada the administration has been given in the hands of the Minister who has to undertake, promote and recommend measures for the encouragement of public corporation in wild life conservation and interpretation. They have to undertake the programmes, wild life research and investigation, establish and maintain laboratories for this purpose. They also have to establish advisory committee as the Minister deems necessary. He has to co-ordinate, implement the wild life policies and programmes in cooperation with the government of any province having an interest therein.

In China Article 30 deals with the administrative measures for the wild life under special local protection and for other wild life that is not under special state protection. This is formulated by the of the standing committee of the people's provinces, autonomous regions and congresses municipalities directly under the central government.

In Japan Article 1-2 says that the Prefectural Governor will have to abide by the standard specified by the Director General of the Environment Agency upon hearing the opinion of the Nature Conservation Council. In this part he has to provide certain specifications like the term of plan, matters regarding establishing of sanctuaries, provision regarding temporary hunting in prohibited area, etc. He has to look into the matter regarding artificial propagation of game, survey of habitat of the game, public information, development of steps to workout the game, protection, project and other necessary matter for execution of the game protection project.

In Malawi Section 5 of Malawi National Parks and Wild Life Act (1992) tells us that there has to be one officer as Chief Park and Wild Life Officer and some subordinate officer will be responsible for administration; subject to any general and special direction given by the Minister.

Article 6.1 says that it is the Minister who is responsible for the National Park and Wild Life in the country of Malawi. It is also observed that every officer shall exercise those duties as conferred upon them by this Act. I have noticed that there is Wild Life Research and Management Board which is set-up to advice the Minister on all matter relating to national park and wild life management in Malawi. The administrative provisions of different countries when compared with that of India discovered that in India too various authorities are responsible for the administration of the different categories of the protected areas. In India the authorities are named as, Collector, Chief Wild Life Warden, police officers and other forest officers.

(7) Penal Provisions

My observations will not be complete without specific mention of the sanctions/punishment given to those persons who have violated any law, which is made for the protection and administration of wild life. After examining the provisions for penalty, one can say that there is very little difference with regard to the basic provisions of punishment and the wrong doer is not spared at any cost. Bulgaria has this provision laid down under Section 2 of Article 81 of the Act. Here the penalties vary on the basis of the categories like natural persons, officials, sole traders or natural legal persons. Article 85 further says that any violation done under Articles 82, 83, 84 shall be established with a writ issued by an official. The penal ordinances shall be issued by different Ministers and officers or authorised persons. Section 2 of Article 85 says, a violation of Article 83 or 82 will be punishable by official person nominated by the Minister. Appeal laid down in Section 3 of Article 85 would be under the Procedure Act. Article 86 further gives the provision for compensation caused for the guilty.

Coming to Canada, here also the punishment is given to the wrong doer. The punishment is in term of fine as well as imprisonment or both. The punishment may vary: (a) in the case of a corporation, to a fine not exceeding $ 250,000, and (b) in the case of an individual, to a fine not exceeding $100,000. The imprisonment may vary from six months to five years. There is also a provision for subsequent offence and continuing offence.

Coming to China Article 31 says that anyone who illegally catches or harms or kills the wild life under the Special State protection shall be prosecuted for criminal responsibility. It further says that if the circumstances are serious enough to constitute a crime, he shall be prosecuted for criminal responsibility in accordance with the provisions of Article 130 of the Criminal Law of China. Similarly Articles 33 to 37 deals with the punishments provided.

In Japan also, like the other 3 countries mentioned above, the wrong doer is liable to a penal servitude which can be in the form of fine or imprisonment or both. The variation in the fine lies between ten thousand to fifty thousand yen.

In Malawi all punishment levied upon the wrong doer is recovered as a civil debt owned to the government. They have liquidated fine and imprisonment upto 5 years.

In India the Penal provision is laid down in the name of prevention and detention of offences which are given under Section 50 to 58 of the Wild Life (Protection) Act, 1972.

Thus it is observed that in China the first onous lies in the hands of the department of Wild Life Administration to penalise the wrong doer and in case of grave violations the punishment is imposed under and in accordance to their criminal laws. It is noteworthy to observe that the maximum punishment as regards the imprisonment is in India which extends to 7 years. Like any other country mentioned above, India is no exception in this regard though the penalising statutes reveal that the punishments vary from person to person i.e. legal persons, natural persons, etc. My observations revealed the fact that in other countries there is no specific mention of cognizable or non-cognizable offences whereas the Indian Wild Life Act has made provisions in this regard also.

(8) Settlement of Tribal Rights

The objective of Wild Life Laws and their Impact on Tribes", would be incomplete without the mention of Tribal Rights which have been covered to some extent in this chapter under the subtitle Settlement of Tribal Rights. The Act of Bulgaria reveals that no direct mention of the rights of the tribes is made in it, but Article-II of the Act indirectly point out that the rights of the owners and users of forest exist as per the protected area declaration order and also with the management plan, regardless of the permits required under other laws.

In Canada the Section 3 on Aboriginal and Treaty rights says: "For greater certainty, nothing in this Act shall be construed so as to abrogate or derogate from any existing aboriginal or treaty rights of the aboriginal peoples of Canada under Section 35 of the Constitution Act, 1982." This section throws light on the provisions for the existing aboriginal or treaty rights of the aboriginal people of Canada. In the Wild Life Act of China no such reference of tribal rights has been made. When compared with that of Japan it was found that to protect the person who has a right of ownership or other rights with respect to the land or standing areas inside the boundary of the sanctuary, the power is vested in the Director-General of the Environment Agency or the Prefectural Governor to establish a special sanctuary inside of the boundary of the sanctuary. The study of the Wild Life Act of Malawi shows that no direct reference of the settlement of tribal rights has been made in it.

The study of the Wild Life Acts of the various countries for the settlement of the tribal rights point out that although the term tribe is not used while stating the rights of the owners and users of forests and lands within the protected areas but it could be interpreted in favour of tribes because of the well known fact that protected areas are mostly populated by tribes.

Coming to India, we can observe the settlement of the rights of tribes which are as follows: (1) Section 65 of the Wild Life Protection Act of India protects the hunting rights of the scheduled tribes of Andaman and Nicobar Islands. (2) Section 24 of the same Act gives power to the Collector to admit or reject the rights within the sanctuary. In the case of National Parks no such privilege is given. There is also a mention that the tribal people will be compensated, after their lands have been taken away by the State, in the form of either settling them in different places and making arrangements for them for ploughing their lands.

Notes and References

1. http://sdnp-delhi.nie.in/resourees/wildlife/wildlife—france. html
2. http://sdnp-delhi.nie.in/resourees/wildlife/wildlife—france. html
3. V.N. Shukla, *Constitution of India,* (Lucknow: Eastern Book Company, 2001) A25.
4. Sanjay Upadhyay and Ashish Kothari, *National Parks and Sanctuaries in India,* (Allahabad: Print World, 2001) 1.

3

Laws Relating to the Rights of the Tribes in India

According to Encyclopaedia Britannica the term tribe in cultural anthropology, means:

> a theoretical type of human social organisation based on small groups defined by tradition of common descent and having temporary or permanent political integration above the family level and a shared language, culture and ideology.[1]

Tribes are ethnic groups having their own customs, cultures, lifestyles, etc., and they are different from the non-tribal people. They form their own social organisation according to their own needs and requirements.

The first attempt to list these communities as primitive tribes was made during the census of 1931. In the Government of India Act (1935) a reference was made to "Backward Tribes" and again the Thirteenth Schedule to the Government of India (Provincial Legislative Assemblies) Order, 1936, specified certain tribes as backward. The Indian Constitution, which came into force on 26 January 1950, for the first time gave the term "Scheduled Tribe" for the tribes.

Today the tribal people are classified under the Fifth and Sixth Schedules of the Constitution of India. They live in different parts of the country and in a variety of geographical regions, over an area extending from North-East through Chotanagpur plateau and Central India to Western India.

Dr. K.S. Singh studies the situation of the tribes in his article, "The Tribal Situation in India", in which he reveals that the term Scheduled Tribe has not been defined in the Constitution of India. The notion of a tribe in India is determined on the basis of the directives given to the State for their welfare and upliftment as they live in those areas like hills and forests, which are considered backward in terms of development. Hence the Scheduled Tribes gain their identity on the parameters of relative isolation and backwardness.

Although the term Scheduled Tribe is not defined under the Indian Constitution but schedule V and VI of the Constitution has enlisted some tribes as Scheduled Tribes. They are known under various names like *Adivasis,* Aboriginals, Backwards, Primitives, *Vanavasis,* etc. There is no universally accepted term as such for them. Dependent on the natural resources the tribal people have been leading a simple life. In India these groups are not new, they have their place in our ancient epics like Mahabharata and Ramayana. The cultural, social, economical and political values of tribes are different from our civilized society.

According to 1991 census survey, India's population contains approximately 8.8% of the Scheduled Tribes. They are commonly known as *'Janjati'*, *'Vanyajati'*, *'Adivasi'* etc. The tribes belong to all of the major language families, the Indo-Aryan, the Dravidian, the Austro-Asiatic, the Tibeto-Burman and the Andamanese. Even though racial categories have been discarded, the tribes are drawn from categories such as the Negrito, Protoaustraloid, Mongoloid and Caucasoid on the basis of the variation in their morphological and genetic traits. They are also differentiated on the basis of the diversities in languages, linguistic traits, ecological situations, cultural characteristics, demographic and biological traits. This shows their heterogeneous nature differing from one another in language, culture and physical features and also reveals their ancient tradition. Being the ethnic minorities of India they required special attention. This attention was given to them in the form of special laws since the British period.

In India there are five tribal regions with a wide range of variations in terms of population density, level and pace of change and development and social formations including political and agrarian check. The foremost policies, which were adopted by the British rulers, were to isolate tribes from the masses and separate the tribal areas from the purview of the general administration.

In fact the area-wise isolation began with the enactment of the Government of India Act of 1870 and a few tracts were specified as Scheduled tracts. In 1874 the Scheduled District Act gave effect to the Government of India Act, 1870 which specified some areas as Scheduled Tracts A number of Acts were enforced from time to time till 1919. Under the Government of India Act in 1919 certain territories were declared Backward Tracts. The areas were more or less with certain additions and omissions the same as those of Scheduled Tracts and Scheduled Districts. Montague and Chelmsford in their report, considered certain areas to be backward, which were later on declared as Backward Tracts.

Under Sections 91 and 92 of the Government of India Act (1935) two areas were created, "Excluded Areas" and "Partially Excluded Areas."

> The list of the areas was embodied in the Government of India (Excluded and Partially Excluded Areas) Order, 1936. On the whole the list of excluded areas or partially excluded areas largely left the situation as it was in 1874 barring only certain areas on the then frontiers. The main features to distinguish an Excluded Area from a Partially Excluded Area were: (i) the Governor functioned in his own discretion in an 'excluded area' whereas he sought the advice of the ministers in a 'partially excluded area,' (ii) the expenditure in regard to the former was non-votable while the demands in the latter case were subject to a vote of the Legislature, (iii) the discussion of any matter regarding the excluded areas needed prior consent of the Governor.[2]

This reveals that by establishing some areas as Back Tracts from time to time, Britishers left the tribe for self governance as a result of which the primitive society was deprived of the protection of any political institution. The British Parliament was eager enough to show that something had been done to help the tribal people through special administration in the areas concerned. But it was only a mockery on the part of the Britishers to help the trial people with special protections in these demarcated areas.

After Independence India's first Prime Minister Jawaharlal Nehru thought over the condition of the tribals and tried to maintain a balance between two aspects, i.e. to retain the identity of the tribes people and at the same time not to isolate them from the masses. The objective of the government should be the all round development of the tribes in relation to the society by establishing and organic link between the tribes, people and the masses.

Addressing an All-India Conference of the tribals held at Jagdalpur (Bastar District, Madhya Pradesh) in March, 1955, Nehru advised his tribal brethren in the following words:

> Wherever you live, you should live in your own way. This is what I want you to decide yourselves. How would you like to live? Your old customs and habits are good. We want that they should survive but at the same time we want that you should be educated and should do your part in the welfare of our country (Nehru, 1955).[3]

Another line of thought which emphasized on the rapid integration of the tribal people with the general population and the pioneer in this regard was given by the Scheduled Area and Scheduled Tribe Commission (S.A. and S.T. Commission). A Study team on tribal development programmes (1969) felt that target set by the S.A. and S.T. Commission, of total assimilation by the end of the Fourth Five Year Plan, is some what optimistic. Though it was in agreement with the view of the Commission that the social and economic advancement should be accelerated; the team considered the factors that militate against progress in large number and after reviewing the position it reached another line of thought more or less similar to that of the S.A. and S.T. Commission with slight modifications.

The National Park Policy of Britishers i.e., keeping the tribes outside the Protected Areas are still persistent even after

Independence and the model of free India is also based on that previous policy. The declaration of a few particular areas of tribal concentration as Scheduled Areas and Tribal Areas is again an example of isolation.

The enlisting of the Scheduled Tribes also creates a wrong impression of tribal people being under a special law. Tribals subsist on forest produce, fishing, agriculture and horticulture. As a result of which there was less interaction of the tribal people outside their community. Hence the tribal people became more reserved and hesitant. Therefore there was felt the necessity to establish a link between the tribal people and the so-called cultured society. Late Pandit Jawaharlal Nehru made an integrational approach in this direction for the first time in 1958 by giving "Panchsheel" i.e. five fundamental principles for the tribal upliftment. The principles are:

(i) People should develop along the lines of their own genius and we should avoid imposing anything on them. We should try to encourage in every way their own traditional arts and culture.
(ii) Tribal rights to land and forest should be respected.
(iii) We should try to train and build up a team of their own people to do the work of administration and development. Some technical personnel from outside will no doubt, be needed, especially in the beginning. But we should avoid introducing too many outsiders into tribal territory.
(iv) We should not over administer these areas or overwhelm them with a multiplicity of schemes. We should rather work through, and not in rivalry to, their own social and cultural institutions.
(v) We should judge results, not by statistics or the amount of money spent, but by the quality of human character that is evolved.

From the experience of the working of the 'Panchsheel' for the tribals we find: (i) that we should not force tribals to do things, (ii) that tribal rights aim at saving tribals from exploitation which can be possible only by integrating them with their neighbouring people, (iii) that only tribal officers may work in the area with some local bias, and in these conditions experienced non-tribal officers have proved themselves to be anthropological in approach, (iv) that tribal programmes be very simple, and (v) that one has to 'serve the tribals in a dedicated spirit.'[4]

We have already discussed the British policy of isolation of large tribal areas, which imposed danger for the development of the tribes. The principles laid down under "Panchsheel" made efforts to bring the tribals back to the main stream of the Indian population. The Constitution of India also takes a step forward in this direction by, giving some provisions of general nature which incorporate in themselves the tribal people, and others, which specifically relate to the tribal safeguards, as the reservation of seats in the Parliament, the State Legislature, the Panchayat Raj bodies and reservation in government services. Article 366 of the Indian Constitution gives the meaning of Scheduled Tribes.

Clause 25 of Article 366 defines the Scheduled Tribes as under:

> Scheduled Tribes means such tribes or tribal communities or parts or groups within such tribes or tribal communities as are deemed under Article 342 to be Scheduled Tribes for the purpose of this Constitution.[5]

Although the term Scheduled Tribe is given by the Indian Constitution, the term has been identified by two parameters, that of relative isolation and backwardness.

Various provisions for the welfare of the tribes have been given under the Indian Constitution. To refer to these I have consulted the book *Constitution of India* by V.N. Shukla. Some of the provisions are stated below:

Right to Equality

Article 14. Equality Before Law

The State shall not deny to any person equality before the law or the equal protection of the laws within the territory of India.

Article 15. Prohibition of Discrimination on Grounds of Religion, Race, Caste, Sex or Place of Birth:

(1) The State shall not discriminate against any citizen on grounds only of religion, race, caste, sex, place of birth or any of them.

(2) No citizen shall, on grounds only of religion, race, caste, sex, place of birth or any of them, be subject to any disability, liability, restriction or condition with regard to :

(a) Access to shops, public restaurants, hotels and places of public entertainment; or

(b) The use of wells, tanks, bathing ghats, roads and places of public resort maintained wholly or partly out of State funds or dedicated to the use of the general public.

(3) Nothing in this article shall prevent the State from making any special provision for women and children.

[1][(4) Nothing in this article or in clause (2) of article 29 shall prevent the State from making any special provision for the advancement of any socially and educationally backward classes of citizens or for the Scheduled Castes and the Scheduled Tribes.]

Article 16. Equality of Opportunity in Matters of Public Employment

(1) There shall be equality of opportunity for all citizens in matters relating to employment or appointment to any office under the State.

(2) No citizen shall, on grounds only of religion, race, caste, sex, descent, place of birth, residence or any of them, be ineligible for, or discriminated against in respect of, any employment or office under the State.

(3) Nothing in this article shall prevent Parliament from making any law prescribing, in regard to a class or classes of employment or appointment to an office [2][under the Government of, or any local or other authority within, a State or Union

1. Added by the Constitution (First Amendment) Act, 1951, S. 2.
2. Subs. by the Constitution (Seventh Amendment) Act, 1956. S. 29, and Sch. for "under any State specified in the First Schedule or any local or other authority within its territory, any requirement as to residence within that State"

territory, any requirement as to residence within that State or Union territory] prior to such employment or appointment.

(4) Nothing in this article shall prevent the State from making any provision for the reservation of appointments or posts in favour of any backward class of citizens, which, in the opinion of the State, is not adequately represented in the services under the State.

Right to Freedom

Article 19. Protection of Certain Rights Regarding Freedom of Speech, etc.

(1) All citizens shall have the right—

(a) to freedom of speech and expression;
(b) to assemble peaceably and without arms;
(c) to form associations or Unions;
(d) to move freely throughout the territory of India;
(e) to reside and settle in any part of the territory of India; [3][and]
(f) [4][* * *]
(g) to practise any profession, or to carryon any occupation, trade or business.

These rights are under the reasonable restriction given in clauses 2 to 6 of Article 19 clause 5 of Article 19 is as follows,

Clause 5: "Nothing in [5][sub-clauses (d) and (e)] of the said clause shall effect the operation of any existing law in so far as it imposes, or prevent the State from making any law imposing, reasonable restriction on the exercise of any of the rights conferred by the said sub-clauses either in the interests of the general public or for the protection of the interest of any Scheduled Tribe."

3. Ins. By Constitution (Forty-forth Amendment) Act, 1978, S. 2 (w.e.f. 20-6-1979).
4. Clause(f) on "to acquire, hold and dispose of property; and" moitted by Constitution (Forth-fourth Amendment) Act, 1978, S. 2 (w.e.f. 20-6-1979).]
5. Subs. by the Constitution (Forty-fourth Amendment), Act, 1978, S. 2 for "sub-clauses (d), (e) and (f)" (w.e.f. 20-6-1979).]

Article 25. Freedom of conscience and free profession, practice and propagation of religion

(1) Subject to public order, morality and health and to the other provisions of this part, all persons are equally entitled to freedom of conscience and the right freely to profess, practice and propagate religion.

Cultural and Educational Rights

Article 29. Protection of Interests of Minorities

(1) Any section of the citizens residing in the territory of India or any part thereof having a distinct language, script or culture of its own shall have the right to conserve the same.

(2) No citizen shall be denied admission into any educational institution maintained by the State or receiving aid out of State funds on grounds only of religion, race, caste, language or any of them.

Article 30. Right of Minorities to Establish and Administer Educational Institutions

(1) All minorities, whether based on religion or language, shall have the right to establish and administer educational institutions of their choice.

[6][(IA) In making any law providing for the compulsory acquisition of any property of an educational institution established and administered by a minority, referred to in clause (1), the State shall ensure that the amount fixed by a or determined under such law for the acquisition of such property is such as would not restrict or abrogate the right guaranteed under that clause.]

(2) The State shall not, in granting aid to educational institutions, discriminate against any educational institution on the ground that it is under the management of a minority, whether based on religion or language.

Directive Principles of State Policy

Article 46. Promotion of educational and economic interests of Scheduled Castes, Scheduled Tribes and other weaker sections : The

6. Ins. by the Constitution (Forty-fourth Amendment) Act, 1978, S. 4 (w.e.f. 20-6-1979).

State shall promote with special care the educational and economic interests of the weaker sections of the people, and in particular, of the Scheduled Castes and the Scheduled Tribes, and shall protect them from social injustice and all forms of exploitation.

State Council of Ministers

Article 164. Other Provisions as to Ministers

(1) The Chief Minister shall be appointed by the Governor and the other Ministers shall be appointed by the Governor on the advice of the Chief Minister, and the Ministers shall hold office during the pleasure of the Governor:

Provided that in the State of Bihar, Madhya Pradesh and Orissa, there shall be a Minister in charge of tribal welfare who may in addition be in charge of the welfare of the Scheduled Castes and backward classes or any other work.

The Scheduled and Tribal Areas all Capital

Article 244. Administration of Scheduled Areas and Tribal Areas

(1) The provisions of the Fifth Schedule shall apply to the administration and control of the Scheduled Areas and Scheduled Tribes in any State [7][* * *] other than [8][the States of Assam [9][Meghalaya, Tripura and Mizoram]].

(2) The provisions of the Sixth Schedule shall apply to the administration of the tribal areas in [10][the States of Assam [11][Meghalaya, Tripura and Mizoram]].

---

7. The words and letters "specified in Part A or Part B of the First Schedule" omitted by the Constitution (Seventh Amendment) Act, 1956, S. 29 and Sch.
8. Subs. by the North-Eastern Areas (Reorganisation) Act, 1971 (81 of 1971), S. 71 for "the State of Assam" (w.e.f. 21.1.1972).
9. Subs. by the State of Mizoram Act, 1986 for "Meghalaya and Tripura" subs. by Constitution (Forth-ninth Amendment) Act, 1984 (w.e.f. 1.4.1984).]
10. Subs. by the North-Eastern Areas (Reorganisation) Act, 1971 (81 of 1971), S. 71 for "the State of Assam" (w.e.f. 21.1.1972).
11. Subs. by the State of Mizoram Act, 1986 for, "Meghalaya and Tripura" subs. by Constitution (Forth-month Amendment) Act, 1984 (w.e.f. 1.4.1984).]

[12]Article 244-A Formation of an autonomous State comprising certain tribal areas in Assam and creation of local Legislature or Council of Ministers or both therefore:

(1) Notwithstanding anything in this constitution, Parliament may, by law, form within the State of Assam an autonomous State Comprising (whether wholly or in part) all or any of the tribal areas specified in [13][part I] of the table appended to paragraph 20 of the Sixth Schedule and create therefore :

(a) a body, whether elected or partly nominated and partly elected, to function as a Legislature for the autonomous State, or
(b) a Council of Ministers, or both with such constitution, powers and functions, in each case, as may be specified in the law.

(2) Any such law as is referred to in clause (1) may, in particular—

(a) specify the matters enumerated in the State List or the Concurrent List with respect to which the Legislature of the autonomous State shall have power to make laws for the whole or any part thereof, whether to the exclusion of the Legislature of the State of Assam or otherwise;
(b) define the matters with respect to which the executive power of the autonomous State shall extend;
(c) provide that any tax levied by the State of Assam shall be assigned to the autonomous State in so far as the proceeds thereof are attributable to the autonomous State;
(d) provide that any reference to a State in any article of this Constitution shall be construed as including a reference to the autonomous State; and
(e) make such supplemental, incidental and consequential provisions as' may be deemed necessary.

12. Ins. by the Constitution (Twenty-second Amendment) Act, 1969, S. 2.]
13. Subs. by the North-Eastern Areas (Reorganisation) Act, 1971 (81 of 1971), S. 71, for "Part A" (w.e.f. 21.1.1972).]

(3) An amendment of any such law as aforesaid in so far as such amendment relates to any of the matters specified in sub-clause (a) or sub-clause (b) of clause (2) shall have no effect unless the amendment is passed in each House of Parliament by not less that two-thirds of the members present and voting.

(4) Any such law as is referred to in this article shall not be deemed to be an amendment of this Constitution for the purposes of Article 368 notwithstanding that it contains any provisions which amends or has the effect of a amending this Constitution.

Article 249. Power of Parliament to Legislate with Respect to a Matter in the State List in the National Interest

(1) Notwithstanding anything in the foregoing provisions of this Chapter, if the Council of States has declared by resolution supported by not less than two-thirds of the members present and voting that it is necessary or expedient in national interest that Parliament should make laws with respect to any matter enumerated in the State List specified in the resolution, it shall be lawful for Parliament to make laws for the whole or any part of the territory of India with respect to that matter while the resolution remains in force.

Article 275. Grants from the Union to Certain States

(1) Such sums as Parliament may by law provide shall be charged on the Consolidated Fund of India in each year as grants-in-aid of the revenues of such States as Parliament may determine to be in need of assistance, and different sums may be fixed for different States:

> Provided that there shall be paid out of the Consolidated Fund of India as grants-in-aid of the revenues of a State such capital and recurring sums as may be necessary to enable that State to meet the costs of such schemes of development as may be undertaken by the State with the approval of the Government of India for the purpose of promoting the welfare of the Scheduled Tribes in that State or raising the level of administration of the Scheduled Areas therein to that of the administration of the rest of the areas of that State;

SPECIAL PROVISIONS RELATING TO CERTAIN CLASSES

Article 330. Reservation of seats for Scheduled Castes and Scheduled Tribes in the House of the People

(1) Seats shall be reserved in the House of the People for—

(a) the Scheduled Castes;

[14][(b) the Scheduled Tribes except the Scheduled Tribes in the autonomous districts of Assam; and]

(c) the Scheduled Tribes in the autonomous districts of Assam.

(2) The number of seats reserved in any State [15][or Union Territory] for the Scheduled Castes or the Scheduled Tribes under clause (1) shall bear, as nearly as may be, the same proportion to the total number of seats allotted to that State [15][or Union Territory] in the House of the People as the population of the Scheduled Castes in the State [15](or Union Territory) or of the Scheduled Tribes in the State [15](or Union Territory), or part of the State 2 (or Union Territory), as the case may be, in respect of which seats are so reserved, bears to the total population of the State [15](or Union Territory).

[16][(3) Notwithstanding anything contained in clause (2), the number of seats reserved in the House of the People for the Scheduled Tribes in the autonomous districts of Assam shall bear to the total number of seats allotted to that State a proportion not less than the population of the Scheduled Tribes in the said autonomous districts bears to the total population of the State.]

[17][Explanation—In this article and in article 332, the expression "population" means the population as ascertained at the last preceding census of which the relevant figures have been published:

14. Subs. by the Constitution (Fifty-first Amendment) Act, 1984, S. 2(1) (w.e.f. 16.6.1986).
15. Ins. by the Constitution (Seventh Amendment) Act, 1956, S. 29 and Sch.).
16. Ins. by the Constitution (Thirty-first Amendment) Act, 1973, S. 3.
17. Ins. by the Constitution (Forty-second Amendment) Act, 1976, S. 47.

Provided that the reference in this Explanation to the last preceding census of which the relevant figures have been published shall, until the relevant figures for the first census taken after the year 2000 have been published, be construed as a reference to the 1971 census.]

Article 332. Reservation of Seats for Scheduled Castes and Scheduled Tribes in the Legislative Assemblies of the State

(1) Seats shall be reserved for the Scheduled Castes and the Scheduled Tribes, [18][except the Scheduled Tribes in the autonomous districts of Assam] in the Legislative Assembly of every State[19] [* * *]

(2) Seats shall be reserved also for the autonomous districts in the Legislative Assembly of the State of Assam.

(3) The number of seats reserved for the Scheduled Castes or the Scheduled Tribes in the Legislative Assembly of any State under clause (I) shall bear, as nearly as may be, the same proportion to the total number of seats in the Assembly as the population of the Scheduled Castes in the State or of the Scheduled Tribes in the State or part of the State, as the case may be, in respect of which seats are so reserved, bears to the total population of the State.

Article 334. Reservation of seats and special representation to cease after [20][sixty years]- Notwithstanding anything in the foregoing provisions of this Part, the provisions of this Constitution relating to

(a) the reservation of seats for the Scheduled Castes and the Scheduled Tribes in the House of the People and in the Legislative Assemblies of the States; and

---

18. Subs. for the words "except the Schedule Tribes in the Tribal areas of Assam, in Nagaland and in Meghalaya" where the words "and in Nagaland" had been added by the Constitution (Twenty-third Amendment) Act, 1969 and "and in Meghalaya" added by the Constitution (Thirty-first Amendment) Act, 1973 by the Constitution (Forty-first Amendment) Act, 1984, S. 3(1) (w.e.f. 16.6.1986).
19. The words and letters "specified in Part A or Part B of the First Schedule" omitted by the Constitution (Seventh Amendment) Act, 1956, S. 29 and Sch.
20. Subs. by the Constitution (Seventy-Ninth Amendment) Act, 1999, S. 2, for "fifty years" (w.e.f. 25.1.2000).

(b) the representation of the Anglo-Indian community in the House of the People and in the Legislative Assemblies of the States by nomination, shall cease to have effect on the expiration of a period of [21][sixty years] from the commencement of this Constitution:

Provided that nothing in this article shall affect any representation in the House of the People or in the Legislative Assembly of a State until the dissolution of the then existing House or Assembly, as the case may be.

Article 335. Claims of Scheduled Castes and Scheduled Tribes to Services and Posts

The claims of the members of the Scheduled Castes and the Scheduled Tribes shall be taken into consideration, consistently with the maintenance of efficiency of administration in the making of appointments to services and posts in connection with the affairs of the Union or of a State.

[22][Provided that nothing in this article shall prevent in making of any provision in favour of the members of the Scheduled Castes and the Scheduled Tribes for relaxation in qualifying marks in any examination or lowering the standards of evaluation, for reservation in matters of promotion to any class or classes of services or posts in connection with the affairs of the Union or of a State.]

Article 338. [23][National Commission for Scheduled Castes and Scheduled Tribes

[24][(1) There shall be a commission for the Scheduled Castes and Scheduled Tribes to be known as the National Commission for the Scheduled Castes and Scheduled Tribes.

(2) Subject to the provisions of any law made in this behalf by Parliament, the Commission shall consist of a Chairperson,

21. Subs. by the Constitution (Seventy-Ninth Amendment) Act, 1999, S. 2, for "fifty years" (w.e.f. 25.1.2000).
22. Ins. By Const. (Eighty-second) Amendment Act, 2000, S. 2.
23. Subs. for the margin heading "Special Officer for Scheduled Castes, Scheduled Tribes, etc." by the Constitution (Sixty-fifth Amendment) Act, 1990 (w.e.f. 12.3.1992).
24. Subs. by *Ibid.* (w.e.f. 12.3.1992).

Vice-Chairperson and five other Members and the conditions of service and tenure of office of the Chairperson, Vice-Chairperson and other Members so appointed shall be such as the President may by rule determine.

(3) The Chairperson, Vice-Chairperson and other Members of the Commission shall be appointed by the President by warrant under his hand and seal.

(4) The Commission shall have the power to regulate its own procedure.

(5) It shall the be duty of the Commission :

(a) to investigate and monitor all matters relating to the safeguards provided for the Scheduled Castes and Scheduled Tribes under this Constitution or under any other law for the time being in force or under any order of the Government and to evaluate the working of such safeguards;

(b) to inquire into specific complaints with respect to the deprivation of rights and safeguards of the Scheduled Castes and Scheduled Tribes;

(c) to participate and advise on the planning process of socio-economic development of the Scheduled Castes and Scheduled Tribes and to evaluate the progress of their development under the Union and any State;

(d) to present to the President, annually and at such other times as the Commission may deem fit, reports upon the working of those safeguards;

(e) to make in such reports recommendations as to the measures that should be taken by the Union or any State for the effective implementation of those safeguards and other measures for the protection, welfare and socio-economic development of the Scheduled Castes and Scheduled Tribes; and

(f) to discharge such other functions in relation to the protection, welfare and development and advancement of the Scheduled Castes and Scheduled Tribes as the President may, subject to the provisions of any law made by Parliament, by rule specify.

(6) The President shall cause all such reports to be laid before each House of Parliament along with a memorandum explaining the action taken or proposed to be taken on the recommendations relating to the Union and the reasons for the non-acceptance, if any, of any of such recommendations.

(7) Where any such report, or any part thereof, relates to any matter with which any State Government is concerned, a copy of such report shall be forwarded to the Governor of the State who shall cause it to be laid before the Legislature of the State along with a memorandum explaining the action taken or proposed to be taken on the recommendations relating to the State and the reasons for the non-acceptance, if any, of any of such recommendations.

(8) The Commission shall, while investigating any matter referred to in sub-clause (a) or inquiring into any complaint referred to in sub-clause (b) of clause (5) have all the powers of a civil court trying a suit and in particular in respect of the following matters, namely:

(a) summoning and enforcing the attendance of any person from any part of India and examining him on oath;
(b) requiring the discovery and production of any document;
(c) receiving evidence on affidavits;
(d) requisitioning any public record or copy thereof from any court of office;
(e) issuing commissions for the examination of witnesses and documents;
(f) any other matter which the President may, by rule, determine.

(9) The Union and every State Government shall consult the Commission on all major policy matters affecting Scheduled Castes and Scheduled Tribes.]

[25][(10)] In this article references to the Scheduled Castes and Scheduled Tribes shall be construed as including references to such other backward classes as the President may, on receipt of

25. Clause (3) renumbered as clause (10) by *Ibid*.

the report of a Commission appointed under clause (1) of Article 340, by order specify and also to the Anglo-Indian community.

Article 339. Control of the Union over the administration of Scheduled Areas and the welfare of Scheduled Tribes

(1) The President may at any time and shall, at the expiration of ten years from the commencement of this Constitution by order appoint a Commission to report on the administration of the Scheduled Areas and the welfare of the Scheduled Tribes in the State[26] [* * *]

The order may define the composition, powers and procedure of the Commission and may contain such incidental or ancillary provisions, as the President may consider necessary or desirable.

(2) The executive power of the Union shall extend to the giving of directions to [27][a State] as to the drawing up of the execution of schemes specified in the direction to be essential for the welfare of the Scheduled Tribes in the State.

Article 342. Scheduled Tribes

(1) The President [28][may with respect to any State 2 (or Union territory), and where it is a state[29] [* * *], after consultation with the Governor [30][* * *] thereof,] by public notification,[31] specify the tribes or tribal communities or parts of or groups within tribes or tribal communities which shall for the purposes of this Constitution be deemed to be Scheduled Tribes in relation to that State [or Union territory, as the case may be].

(2) Parliament may; by law include in or exclude from the list of Scheduled Tribes specified in a notification issued under clause (1) any tribe or tribal community or part of or group within

26. The words and letters "specified in Part A or Part B of the First Schedule" omitted by the Constitution (Seventh Amendment) Act, 1956, S. 29 and Sch.
27. Subs. by S. 29 and Sch., *Ibid*, for "any such State".
28. Subs. by the Constitution (First Amendment) Act, 1951, S. 11, for "may, after consultation with the Governor or Rajpramukh of a State".
29. Also see Glanter *op. cit.*, Ch. 9.
30. S. Swvigaradoss *v.* Zonal Manager, FCI, (1996) 3 SCC 100: AIR 1996 SC 1182.
31. Subs. by the Constitution (First Amendment) Act, 1951 S. 11, for "may, after consultation with the Governor or Rajpramuk of a State".

any tribe or tribal community, but save as aforesaid a notification issued under the said clause shall not be varied by any subsequent notification.

Article 347. Special Provision Relating to Language Spoken by a Section of the Population of a State

On a demand being made in that behalf the President may, if he is satisfied that a substantial proportion of the population of a State desire the use of any language spoken by them to be recognised by that State, direct that such language shall also be officially recognised throughout that State or any part thereof for such purpose as he may specify.

Special Directives

Article 350. Language to be used in Representations for Redress of Grievances

Every persons shall be entitled to submit a representation for the redress of any grievance to any officer or authority of the Union or a State in any of the languages used in the Union or in the State, as the case may be.

Article[32] 350A. Facilities for Instruction in Mother-tongue at Primary Stage

It shall be the endeavour of every State and of every local authority within the state to provide adequate facilities for instruction in the mother-tongue at the primary stage of education to children belonging to linguistic minority groups; and the President may issue such directions to any State as he considers necessary or proper for securing the provision of such facilities.]

Article 350B. Special Officer for Linguistic Minorities

(1) There shall be a special officer for linguistic minorities to be appointed by the President.

(2) It shall be the duty of the Special Officer to investigate all matters relating to the safeguards provided for linguistic minorities under this Constitution and report to the President

32. Ins. by the Constitution (Seventh Amendment) Act, 1956, S. 21.

upon those matters at such intervals as the President may direct, and the President shall cause all such reports to be laid before each House of Parliament, and set to the Government of the States concerned.]

Article 366. Definitions

In this Constitution, unless the context otherwise requires, the following expressions have the meanings hereby respectively assigned to them, that is to say—Clause (25) "Scheduled Tribes" means such tribes or tribal communities or parts of or groups within such tribes or tribal communities as are deemed under Article 342 to be Scheduled Tribes for the purposes of this Constitution;

The Constitution (Scheduled Castes) orders (Amendment) Act, 1990.

It is an Act passed in order to amend the Constitution (Scheduled Castes) Orders, 1950 and the Constitution (Scheduled Castes) Union Territories Order, 1951 and to amend the Constitution (Jamma and Kashmir) Scheduled Caste Order, 1956 The Constitution (Dadra and Nagar Haveli) Scheduled Castes Order 1962, Order, 1964 and the Constitution (Sikkim Scheduled Castes Order, 1978).

Certain rules for the constitution of the Commission for Scheduled Castes and Scheduled Tribes, their functions and responsibilities, method of investigation and inquiry as well as the interaction of the Commission with the State Government need to be mentioned here. For this the book on The Law Relating to Human Rights (2000) by B.L. Bansal has been consulted.

Rules of Procedure of the National Commission for Scheduled Castes and Scheduled Tribes

1. *Constitution of the Commission*

The National Commission for Scheduled Castes and Scheduled Tribes (hereinafter—called the Commission) has been constituted under Article 338 of the Constitution of India as amended by the (Sixty-fifth Amendment) Act, 1990. The Commission shall consist of a Chairperson, a Vice-Chairperson and five other Menmbers.[6]

2. *The Functions and Responsibilities of the Commission as Laid Down in the Constitution are :*

(a) to investigate and monitor all matters relating to the safeguards provided for the Scheduled Castes and Scheduled Tribes under the Constitution or under any other law for the time being in force or under any order of the Government and to evaluate the working of such safeguards;

(b) to inquire into specific complaints with respect to the deprivation of rights and safeguards of the Scheduled Castes and Scheduled Tribes;

(c) to participate and advise on the planning process of socio-economic development of the Scheduled Castes and Scheduled Tribes and to evaluate the progress of their development under the Union and any State;

(d) to present to the President, annually and at such other times as the Commission may deem fit, reports upon the working of those safeguards;

(e) to make in such reports recommendations as to the measures that should be taken by the Union or any State for the effective implementation of those safeguards and other measures for the protection, welfare and socio-economic development of the Scheduled Castes and Scheduled Tribes; and

(f) to discharge such other functions in relation to the protection, welfare and development and advancement of the Scheduled Castes and Scheduled Tribes as the President may, subject to the provisions of any law made by Parliament, by rule specify.[7]

Division of Responsibilities and Allocation of Work

3. *Chairperson*

(a) The Chairperson shall be the head of the Commission and shall have the residuary powers to decide on all questions and matters arising in the Commission excepting such matters where specific provision has been made in these rules.

(b) The Chairperson shall allocate subjects and responsibilities among the Members of the Commission. The Order allocating the subjects and responsibilities shall be circulated to all concerned by the Secretariat of the Commission.

(c) The Chairperson shall be the authority to sanction leave and approve tours of the Members.

(d) The Chairperson shall preside over the meetings of the Commission.

(e) All important decisions in the Commission pertaining to the subjects allotted to the Members shall be taken with the approval of the Chairperson.

(f) The Chairperson may call for any records on any matter which he considers important and may take a decision on it himself or, if necessary, place it at the meeting of the Commission.[8]

4. *Duties of the State Offices of the Commission*

It shall be the duty of the State Offices of the Commission:

(i) To act as the "eyes and ears" of the Commission in the State(s) of their jurisdiction.

(ii) To maintain effective interaction and liaison with State Government/UT Administrations on behalf of the Commission.

(iii) To serve on State Level Advisory Councils/Committees/Corporations, etc. on behalf of the Commission.

(iv) To provide information and documentation about the policies and programmes of the Union Government for the welfare and advancement of SCs and STs to the States, NGOs, Media in their respective jurisdiction. Obtain similar information and documentation from such organisation and provide to the Headquarters of the Commission information/documentation about important development, social movements, policy changes etc. in the State affecting the interest of SCs and STs.

(v) To monitor and assist the working of voluntary and other non-governmental organisations receiving grants-in-aid from the Ministry of Social Justice and

Empowerment as also other Ministries/Departments of the Central Government and the etc., for Research Studies and any other development work relating to SCs and STs.

(vi) To conduct Research Studies, Seminars, Conferences, Surveys etc. either on their own or as entrusted to them by Headquarters from time to time.

(vii) To conduct on the spot inquiries into cases of atrocities on SCs and STs either on their own or as entrusted to them by Headquarters and interact with the concerned Administrative/Police authorities having jurisdiction and report to the Headquarters.

(viii) To deal with complaints/representations from individuals, SC/ST Welfare Associations, etc. on various matters.

(ix) To participate and advise in the planning process for socio-economic development of the SCs/STs as envisaged under Clause 5 of Article 338 of the Constitution of India.

(x) To collect compile, analyse and monitor issues pertaining to development of SC's and ST's in the State especially with reference to SCP, TSP and SCA, and prepare drafts or reports pertaining to the State/UT under their jurisdiction.

(xi) To prepare and maintain a comprehensive and upto date data base of SC/ST population, education, development etc. in the state/UT; and

(xii) To perform any other duty specifically assigned/entrusted to the State Officer(s) by the Commission or the Secretary or any other officer empowered in this regard.[9]

Broadly speaking human rights may be "regarded as those fundamental and inalienable rights which are essential for life as human being."[10] Human fights are the fights which are possessed by every human being, irrespective of his or her nationality, race, religion, sex etc., simply because he or she is a human being. They are also known as Fundamental Rights; Natural Rights or Basic Right. Indian Constitution has these rights in the name of Fundamental Rights. Tribes are no exception to these rights. The tribal people have been given all these rights and also have other rights which are given under different laws given by the Parliament. Many human rights have been incorporated in the Indian Constitution. Some of those are: Right to life, liberty, equality, Right against arbitrary arrest, Right to freedom of movement, Right to freedom of thought, Right to form and to join trade union etc. Some of the rights which are not specifically mentioned in the Constitution but are declared Human rights by the Supreme Court under the theory of emanation are : Right to Shelter, Right of Compensation, Right to Legal Aid, Right to Privacy, Right to Speedy Trial, Right against Cruel and Unusual Punishment.

There are other laws also for the benefit of the tribes. As it is not practically possible to discuss all those in detail, only a reference to those laws have been made here :

- Bonded Labour System (abolition) Act, 1976.
- The Criminal and Election Laws Amendment Act, 1969.
- The Untouchability (offences) Amendment and Miscellaneous Provision Act, 1973.
- Amendment of the Representation of the People Act, 1951.
- The Protection of Civil Rights Act, 1955.

Legal Aid to Tribes

Without Legal aid the right of the tribal people cannot be enforced. For this purpose by the 42nd amendment in our Constitution a new Article 39A was inserted which states: The State shall secure that the operation of the legal system promotes justice, on the basis of equal opportunity, and shall, in particular, provide free legal aid, by suitable legislation or schemes or in any other way, to ensure that opportunities for securing justice are not denied to any citizen by reason of economic or other disabilities.

In the pursuance of this article Parliament has passed the Legal Services Authorities Act, 1987. Many legal aid centres have been established in our country, but the benefit of those legal aid centres are limited to the urban areas only. Actually tribal populated villages are not able to derive the benefit of these legal aid centres. Reasons behind it are unawareness, illiteracy and non-publicity of programmes.

In the post-Independence period several efforts have been made to improve the state of the weaker sections of the Indian population or to assimilate them with the rest of the population. The Government of India is keen on helping the tribes and is moving ahead with her programmes to sustain the Constitutional safeguards given to them. On the eve of the Fifth Five Year Plan the Parliamentary Forum organized a National Seminar on "Problems and Prospects of Tribal Development in India". In the Fifth Five year Plan introduction of the "Sub-Plan" policy for total and integrated development of different tribal areas has been the out-come of different discussions. These clearly reveal the aims and efforts made by the Government in this direction.

Various programmes or scheme that the Government of India has undertaken for the welfare of tribes are related to their development in the area of economic, cultural, educational, Political, health and sanitation, communication, housing, etc. The amount spent or being spent on them as given below, in the different Plans, itself tells the story of the welfare of the backward classes.

Till the beginning of the Fourth Five Year Plan a total sum of Rs. 375 crores had been spend by the Union and State Governments on the welfare of backward classes. The State Governments, contributed nearly 100 crores from their own resources, during this period. The expenditure incurred exclusively for the Scheduled Tribe as compared to the total expenditure and per capital expenditure under the various Plans gives rise to the fact that the progress is very slow. In the Fifth Five Year Plan, however, the additional allotment or Rs. 500 crores has changed the picture to some extent, which is a healthy sign. The total per capita expenditure till the Fifth Plan comes to Rs. 221.25 only.

Problems of the Tribes People

Many studies on tribes have revealed that they are introvert by nature. The study on "Tribals in a Metropolitan region" by V.S. Phadke and S.S. Pednekar reveals that the tribal people "were very slow to adapt to new situations, and remained uninfluenced by urban shock-waves even when they lived in the peripheries of the metropolitan regions."[11]

They are the much-neglected sections of the society. The literacy level, school enrolment figures at various levels reflect that education level is very low in their community. "Within these 40 years of independence the achievement in tribal education even at the elementary level, not to speak of at high levels, is miserable."[12]

They are deprived of those skills, which are required to earn livelihood and tackle their day-to-day problems in the modern scenario. Due to illiteracy and poverty the other communities exploit them. As a result of these their condition is deteriorating:

> The tribal communities today in the country are passing through critical phase in their history. Discontent among them, the result of many injustices heaped on the, both by the government and non-tribal population is increasing day by day. From the time of the British till today the tribals in many areas of the country have rebelled a number of times (there are more than 70 recorded tribal insurgency cases so far in the country) but without any result. Today the tribal areas in the country have become sancturies for extremists and Naxalites.[13]

This has worsened the situation of the tribal people was anti social groups try to terrorise the tribesmen in various ways by exposing them to the various hazards and making them more insecure within their habitants. As most of the tribal population of the country depends upon agriculture as the main source of livelihood it has becomes the basic resource for them. Hence another major problem resulting out of it, which is common to all the tribal communities is the improvement required in the skills of cultivation among the tribes.

> Though there is an urgent need for improving the skills of cultivation among these people, the greater need 'is to put an end to the large scale land alienation taking place among them: This fact is clearly borne out by the Census figures. From Census to Census among these communities, the percentage of landless labour is increasing while the percentage of cultivators to the total tribal population is decreasing. A number of case studies also have recorded

> this trend and almost all the State Governments have passed Land Transfer Regulation Acts to prevent land alienation among the tribals but unfortunately these regulations have failed to put an end to this sorry state of affairs.[14]

The study shows numbers of landless tribesmen have increased. To mitigate this problem among all State Governments have passed Land Transfer Regulation Act. But on the other hand the government itself is acquiring the land of the tribesmen in the name of Sancturies and National Parks. By alienating the tribesmen from their lands, they have uprooted them from their original habitats and limited their access to the available meagre resource base :

> The case of Chenchus and Raj-is also deserves mention. In the case of the Chenchus the government seems to be interested in the development of animal resources in their territory rather than human resources. This is not the author's view but the view of the Chenchus themselves because of the creation of a tiger reserve in there midst. In 1960s the government's half-hearted effort to introduce agriculture a month Chenchus failed. Likewise the government of Uttar Pradesh forced the Raj is to take to agriculture but failed. A few starvation deaths were also reported in this community, the result of losing hold on their traditional habitat and their inability to adapt to new occupations.[15]

The case study emphasises on a very severe problem faced by the tribes due to the alienation and if no effective measures are taken immediately to resolve the problem the same hazardous result can be expected to take place here in M.P.

As no efforts have been made to put a check to the situation prevailing among the tribesmen there condition has deteriorated to such an extent that even starvation deaths have been reported in the other States like Orissa, etc.

Seeing the severity of the problem faced by the tribes one is forced to think about the measures, which could be taken for the upliftment of these communities. The first important measure is to raise the literacy level and to develop those skill, which will help them to earn their own livelihood.

Another genuine problem of the tribal people, which needs attention, is the alienation and the "entitlement of the tribals. The question arises as to what resources are the tribals entitled ?"[16]

G. Prakash Reddy in an article on "HRD in the tribals," has made a thorough study of the problems and offered solution. Another question, which comes to our one's mind here is that whether the tribesmen hold proprietary rights over a particular habitat by virtue of their birth in there habitats? Several efforts through H.R.D. programmes have been made to solve their problems. These programmes have not been very successful in their attempts:

> It means that the human resource development programmes for these people have to tackle both intangible and tangible aspects. The intangible include creation of will for survival particularly in the case of food gathering communities like Onges and Shompens of Andaman and Nicobar Islands, otherwise the downward trend in their population cannot be stopped, this is a priority area. Secondly, all the tribals in the country today need building-up to confidence-to fight the injustices perpetrated against them by the traders, businessmen, forest contractors, industrialists and the institution of government and confidence also to face life's new situations as they are being pushed more and more into unfamiliar occupations, environment and avenues of life. Thirdly, a kind of pride in their own culture has to be created. Due to influence of various external and internal factors they are losing their own culture. Any community in the process of losing roots in its own culture will experience a kind of trauma which may further influence other aspects of its life.[17]

The grass-root level approach is essential because natural justice demands it. However it does not mean that the development of higher and competitive skills among the poor section of population should be neglected.

In a recent survey conducted by the Anthropological survey of India under the People of India Project, 461 Tribal

Communities have been identified in India. According to the 1981 census, the population of Scheduled Tribes in the country stands at 51, 628, 638 and constitutes 7.76 of the total population.

Various all-India tribal Conferences have been organized and actively supported by Government of India. They are indirectly creating a new solidarity in tribal India.

There is also indirect control of Parliament on the welfare activities, which are looked after by the Parliamentary Committee on the welfare of Scheduled Castes and Scheduled Tribes. Its functions are :

(i) To consider the repports submitted by the Commissioner for Scheduled Castes and Scheduled Tribes under Article 338 (2) of the Contitution and to report to both the Houses after the measures that should be taken by the Union Government in respect of matters within the purview of the Union Government, including the Administrations of the Union Territories;

(ii) To report to both the Houses on the actions taken by the Union Government and the Administrations of the Union Territories regarding the measures already proposed by the Committee;

(iii) To examine the measures taken by the Union Government to secure due representation of the Scheduled Castes and Scheduled Tribes in services and posts under its control (including appointments in the public sector undertakings, statutory and semi-Government bodies and in the Union Territories) having regard to the provisions of Article 335;

(iv) To report to both the Houses on the working of the welfare programmes for the Scheduled Castes and Scheduled Tribes in the Union Territories;

(v) To consider generally and to report to both the Houses on all matters concerning the welfare of the Scheduled Castes and Scheduled Tribes which fall within the purview of the Union Government including the Administrations of the Union Territories; and

(vi) To examine such matters as may seem fit to the Committee or are specifically referred to it by the House or the Speaker.[18]

Different Commissions have been constituted by the Government to assess and analyse the welfare work. The following account will throw light on the various Commissions and Committees formed. The book on The Tribal Culture of India by L.P. Vidyarthi and Binay Kumar Rai gives details of the various Commissions and Committees which are enlisted below:

- The Criminal Tribes Act Enquiry Committee (1949-50).
- Backward Classes Commission (1953-55).
- Estimates Committee of Parliament (1958-59).
- Study Team on Social Welfare and Welfare of Backward Classes (1958-59).
- Committee on Special Multi-purpose Tribal Blocks (1959-60).
- Scavenging Conditions Enquiry Committee (1957-60).
- Scheduled Areas and Scheduled Tribes Commission (1960-61).
- Study Group on the Welfare of the Weaker Sections of the Village Community (1960-61).
- Special Working Group on Co-operation for Backward Classes (1961-62).
- Advisory Committee on the Revision of the Lists of S.C. and S.T. (1965).
- Committee on Customary Rights of Scavengers, (1965-66).
- Committee on Tribal Economy in Forest Areas (1965-67) Working Group to study the progress of measures for Land Allotment to Scheduled Castes and their representation in Services (1967).
- Committee on Untouchability, Economic and Educational development of Scheduled Castes (1965-69).
- Task Force Committee on development of Tribal areas, 1973.

Approach of Voluntary Agencies

Not only the government but some voluntary agencies are equally concerned with the problems of the tribal people.

Under the approach of voluntary agencies we have social workers, social welfare agencies, social movement agencies, and social reformers, which are working in their upliftment of the weaker sections of our society. It was only after independence that government became more interested in the tribal welfare activities. As the social workers were always associated with the welfare of the tribal people they knew their problems in details. Hence the government, when it came to the execution of welfare schemes among the tribal people, took all help and assistance from these social workers. In this way these organisations made a special place for them and started making recommendations to the government on tribal matters.

Various social agencies at the Central and the State level are associated with the development of the tribes. Due to illiteracy and ignorance the tribal people are not aware of their rights and many times cannot even fight for those rights which have already been given to them. In such situations social agencies represent them in the Courts for their benefit. Hence we see that many cases are being filed by these voluntary agencies for tribes in the form of Public Interest Litigation. By accepting the new concept of Public Interest Litigation the Supreme Court of India has recognised the voluntary agencies as the protectors of the weaker sections. This shows the importance of these voluntary agencies in the present times.

Despite all efforts made by these voluntary agencies their urge to work for the tribal welfare does not match their understanding of tribal organization, values and problems.

They sometimes went into the tribal areas with an omnibus solution to the tribal problems as they understood them, while in reality the problems for different tribal groups, and even for section of one tribe, were often different. Their motives were probably laudable in their own cultural frame of reference, but not so against the tribal scheme of values. They failed to realize that their well-intentioned "reforms" may be injurious to the tribes in terms of their socio-cultural life.[19]

Notes and References

1. "Tribe", A New Survey of Universal Knowledge Encyclopaedia Britanica, (Chicago : Inc. William Benton, Publisher, 1965) 465.
2. L.P. Vidyarthi and B.K. Rai, The Tribal Culture of India (New Delhi : Concept Publishing Company, 1985) 418.
3. L.P. Vidyarthi and B.K. Rai, 411.

4. L.P. Vidyarthi and B.K. Rai, 419.
5. The Constitution of India (Delhi : Government of India, Legislative Department, National Language Section, 1991).
6. B.L. Bansal, The Law Relating to Human Rights : The Profection of Human Rights Act, 1993, (Delhi : Capital Law House, 2000) 309.
7. B.L. Bansal, 310.
8. B.L. Bansal, 310-311.
9. B.L. Bansal, 317-318.
10. S.K. Kapoor, International Law and Human Rights (Allahabad : Central Law Agency, 2002) 764.
11. V.S. Phadke, "Tribals in a Metropolitan Region", Social Change : 21.2 (June 1991) 93.
12. G. Prakash Reddy, "HRD in the Tribals," Social Change: 21.2 (June 1991) 93.
13. G. Prakash Reddy, 19.
14. G. Prakash Reddy, 21.
15. G. Prakash Reddy, 22.
16. G. Prakash Reddy, 22-3.
17. L.P. Vidyarthi and B.K. Rai, 424.
18. L.P. Vidyarthi and B.K. Rai, 429.

4

Conflict between the Wild Life Laws and the Laws which Protect the Rights of the Tribes

After a detailed study of the wild life laws of different countries along with that of India in the first and second chapter, I have discussed various laws which protect the rights of the tribes in the third chapter. During the study I have come across certain conflicting provisions which are brought forth in this chapter.

Today environmental (ecological) degradation has become a major cause of concern. Lot of work has been done for the conservation of biological resources by the organisations like IUCN , WWF, UNDP and UNEP. The developing countries have also taken significant interest in the protection of wild life. India also being one of the developing nations has strive for the same.

India has the world's most extensive network of officially protected areas under the Wild Life (Protection) Act, 1972. Due to high population density, changing patterns of life style, developmental pressures and increasing commercialism, the government has taken serious steps towards conservation of wild life, which shows that India's sensitive biological habitats have become a matter of national priority. The term "biological habitat" includes various natural habitats as well as plant and animal species.

As a large number of people depend on these biological resources for their survival, the depletion of the natural resources and likelihood of their further degradation is a matter of worry and concern for everyone in India. Hence there was felt a need for the conservation and protection of these resources. Because the habitat for the tribe and wild animals is the same i.e., the "forests" the problem emerging out of it has to be dealt with a balanced approach.

Although the Wild Life Protection Act, 1972 attempts to settle the rights of the tribal people in an objective manner but sometimes due to certain discrepancies in the laws certain problems are being faced by the tribes. The callous attitude of the environmentalists cannot be ignored here as it becomes another cause for the problems finally resulting into variolus conflicts. "Many of the world's protected areas and areas considered for protection, fall within the territories of indigenous and traditional peoples. However protected areas policies have tended to exclude people from protected areas.

With the government's declaration of certain areas as protected areas, the necessity for the acquisition of lands arises. This leads to the relocation of tribes from their natural habitats which in its turn instils in them the feeling of estrangement and alienation. Therefore we cannot say that the policies of the government for the resettlement of the tribes have been successful.

Hence, it can be stated that the conservation strategies adopted by the government are also responsible, to some extent, for the suffering of the tribes. This has "drawn criticism from human rights groups to the extent that they now sometimes regard the aims of large conservation organisations as in opposition to their own."[2] The approach of the Human Rights group cannot be ignored here, when we talk of the conflicts between the conservation policies to protect the wild life and infringement of the rights of tribes. For a clear understanding of these conflicts, I have categories it into three parts :

(i) Constitutional rights of the tribes *vs*. laws which protect wild life.

(ii) Laws for the protection of rights of the tribes *vs*. wild life laws.

(iii) Critical appraisal of wild life laws.

Let us consider them one by one:

(i) Constitutional Rights of the Tribes v. Laws which Protect Wild Life

First, let us discuss the laws of the tribes given in our Constitution, which come in direct collision with the laws, which protect wild life.

(1) Rights of the Tribal People v. Right to Equality

Section 65 of the Wild Life (Protection) Act states that Rights of Scheduled Tribes have to be protected—Nothing in this Act shall affect the hunting rights conferred on the Scheduled Tribes of the Andaman and Nicobar Islands in the Union Territory of Andaman and Nicobar Islands. This was notified by the notification of the Andaman and Nicobar Administration, No. 40/67/F, No. G 635, Vol. III, dated the 28th April, 1967, published at pages 1 to 5 of the Extraordinary issues of the Andaman and Nicobar Gazette, dated the 28th April, 1967.

But these rights are not conferred on the tribes other than that of the Andaman and Nicobar Islands.

Article 14 of the Indian Constitution confers right to equality and equal protection of law to all persons.

Section 65 of the Wild Life (Protection) Act contradicts Article 14 of the Indian Constitution because it discriminates between the tribes of Andaman and Nicobar Island and the tribes living in other parts of India.

(2) Right to Livelihood v. Prohibition on Livestock Collection

Earlier Article 21 did not include rights of livelihood as was held in Santram,[3] but in the case of Board of Trustee of the Port of Bombay *vs.* Dilipkumar R. Nandkarni,[4] the Supreme Court held that right to livelihood is included in the right to life because "no person can live without the means of living, i.e., the means of livelihood as is held in Olga Tellis *vs.* Bombay Municipal Corporation.[5] In the case of Ramsharan Autyânuprasi *vs.* Union of India,[6] the Supreme Court observed that life includes all that give meaning to a man's life including his traditions, culture, heritage and protection of that heritage in its full measure.

The above provision of the said act expresses absolute prohibition and restriction on rights of the scheduled tribes. After the declaration of certain area as protected area, the inhabitants of that area, who are mostly people belonging to scheduled tribes are displaced from their native places. They have to undergo numberless problems with respect to their habitation and living. They are actually deprived of their property rights. The question of the deprivation of their property rights leading to deprivation of life or liberty or livelihood falls within the reach of Article 21. The Supreme Court in this context has left open the question whether any such deprivation occurs or not. If no such deprivation occurs then Article 21 has no application. The displacement of landowners on acquisition of their land under the Land Acquisition Act, 1894 does not violate Article 21 of the Constitution. But these as has been held in Butu Prasad Kumbhar *vs.* Steel Authority of India Ltd.[7] that the Government in such case shall however provide a suitable scheme for such displaced persons such as employment to one of the members of that family in the plant for which the land is being acquired.

If displaced persons are settled as envisaged by the Supreme Court in the above case then any land acquisition will not be said to be violative of the right to livelihood of a person. But if the settlement process is not in accordance with the directives given by the Supreme Court then it should be treated as violative of Article 21 of the Constitution.

An examination of the situation will lead one to the bare reality that no employment has been given to any family member of the displaced tribes men. Hence one can construe that the enforcement of Wild Life (Protection) Act, in as much as it relates to the acquisition displaced persons, is violative of the Article 21 of the Constitution.

The above provisions show total prohibition and restriction on rights of the tribes. In this way Section 35 infringes the right to livelihood of the tribes which is their fundamental right.

(3) Free Movement v. Restriction on Entry in the Protected Areas

Article 19 (1)(d) of the Indian Constitution states that all citizens shall have the right to move freely throughout the territory of India; and moreover Article 19(5) states that nothing in sub-clause (d) of the said clause shall affect the operation of any existing law in so far as it imposes, or prevents the State from making any law imposing reasonable restrictions on the exercise of any of the rights conferred by the said sub-clause either in the interests of the general public or for the protection of the interests of any Scheduled Tribe.

Section 27 and 35 of the Wild Life (Protection) Act has put restriction on entry in Sanctuary and National Parks with a few exceptions.

This includes restriction of the Scheduled Tribes also to enter into such areas. Article 19(5) provides for the making of law imposing restriction on the right to move freely through the territory of India. But this law has to be in the interest of the general public or for the protection of the interest of the scheduled tribe. Further the Supreme Court talks of the test of the reasonableness to be applied to each individual statute impugned and warns against any abstract standard or general pattern of reasonableness. The second phrase of Article 19(5) "or for the protection of the interests of any scheduled tribe", has to be given cognisance to. To me, it seems, this issue required further analysis. The Government rightly seems to concern itself for the protection and conservation of wild life and environment. But this concernment, if done, at cost of the welfare of the scheduled tribes cannot be said to be justified under the clause of reasonable restriction. The right to free movement of the scheduled tribes is not alone a political Issue but it has to be considered empathetically. The culture, traditions, lifestyle, dietetic habits, medical aid, of the tribesmen is very naturally dependent upon the forests and its produce. The restriction on free movement of the scheduled tribes does not amount to the infringement of their fundamental right to move freely, thereby protect their life and living. Moreover restriction on the movement of the tribesmen in protected areas seems to be violative of Article 19(5), where it says that the imposition of reasonableness should be for the "protection of the interest of the any scheduled tribes."

(4) *Freedom to Reside and Settle v. Restriction on Entry in Sanctuaries and National Parks*

Again, the restriction on entry in Sanctuaries and National Parks, according to section 27 and 35 of Wild Life (Protection) Act, seems to me, to be violative of the provisions of Article 19(e) of the Indian Constitution which states that all citizens shall have the right to reside and settle in any part of the territory of India.

Because, here again the restrictive clause i.e. 19(5) talks of such restriction to be imposed for the protection of the interests of any scheduled tribe", but contrary to this section 27 and 31 of Wild Life (Protection) Act violates the interests of the scheduled tribes.

(5) Cultural Rights v. Relocation

Although title of Article 29 talks of the interest of minorities but it reads that "any section of the citizens residing in the territory of India and any part thereof having a distinct language, script or culture of its own shall have the right to conserve the same". An analysis of the above Article makes one understand that the term "any section" must be applied to all citizens residing in the territory of India and that they have the right to conserve their culture. Therefore the term any section would rightly include scheduled tribes also and that they too have the right to conserve their language, script and culture.

Now, under the Wild Life (Protection) Act, the land is acquired according to the Provision of Land Acquisition 1894. The inhabitants affected by the land acquisition include the scheduled tribes, which are in majority. There are relocated to some place other than the protected areas, many a times the environment of the areas where they are relocated is different from their native place. As a natural consequence to it, it becomes difficult for the tribes men to maintain their cultural activities. No help is provided by the Government to them so as to make them able to preserve and maintain their culture.

In other words, one may say that the Wild (Protection) Act here violates the cultural rights of scheduled tribes as provided in Article 29(l) of Constitution.

(6) Promotion of Economic and Educational Interest v. Restriction on Development

Article 46 of the Constitution provides for the promotion of the educational and economic interests of the weaker section of the people, and in particular, of the scheduled castes and the scheduled tribes. It also provides that the State shall protect these from social injustice and exploitation.

Tribal economy depends primarily on agricultural produce and livestock collection from the forest. When certian areas are declared as protected areas under Sections 18, 35, 36A and 36C of the Wild Life (Protection) Act, the people, most of whom are the scheduled tribes, are relocated. This relocation is generally accomplished in areas which are adjacent to the protected areas. Here against the developmental activities are subject to certain prohibitive conditions. The poor tribesmen, due to paucity of adequate financial resources, are left with no other option but to accept relocation in these areas therefore, once again, due to want of development, the educational and economic interest of the scheduled tribes get hampered.

(7) Wild Life (Protection) Act v. National Commission for Scheduled Tribes and Scheduled Caste

Article 338 of the Constitution of India has declared a National Commission to investigate and monitor all matters relating to the safeguard provided for the scheduled tribes. Under this Constitution or under any other law for time being enforce, or under any order of the Government, and to evaluate the working of such safeguard, the Commission has to report to the President of India about the working of those safeguards and can make recommendations with respect to the measures that should be taken by the various Government for the effective implementation of those safeguard and other measure for the protection, welfare and socio-economic development of the scheduled tribes. The Commission is also authorised to undertake any other functions in relation to the protection, welfare and development of the scheduled tribes as the president may, subject to any law made by the parliament, by rule specify.

An examination of the living conditions of the scheduled tribes and the impact of the enforcement of various laws pertaining to forest areas on them, provides evidence to statement that despite 56 years of freedom of India, Article 338 of the Constitution could not produce the desired result. Various laws were enacted by the Union and different State Governments of the country, which did hamper the welfare prospects of the Scheduled Tribes as envisaged by Article 338 of the Constitution. Little action has been taken by the National Commission or report submitted, with respect to the problems faced by the scheduled tribes when the tribesmen are dislocated due to the declaration of certain forest areas as protected areas, may be under the Wild Life (Protection) Act or the Indian Forest Act.

A critical study of the dislocated tribesmen after the enforcement following acquisition of land under Wild Life (Protection) Act and Indian Forest Act will expose the reality of situation that how many members of the families dislocated, where given employment in the concerned department as directed by the Supreme Court in Butu Prasad Kumbhar *vs*. Steel Authority of India Ltd.[8]

Land acquisition may not be violative of Article 21 of the Indian Constitution if it is followed by suitable scheme of habitation of the displaced persons. But if no such suitable scheme is proposed is or if proposed only on papers, than certainly it is violative of Article 21 of the Constitution.

(ii) Laws for the Protection of the Rights of the Tribes v. Wild Life Laws

After discussion on the constitutional provisions which are in conflict with the wild life laws, I shall now attempt to discover the conflict between the laws which protect the rights of the tribes and the wild life laws.

(1) Intellectual Property Rights of the Tribes v. Protected Areas

All over the world a new concept of rights have been identified and the same has been recognised by the world community. It is known as the Intellectual Property Rights.

In India we know that aboriginal people have numerous concepts in their minds, which can be protected as their intellectual property. One of the most appreciable rights of the tribesmen is naturopathy (Ayurved). It can only be protected when the tribesmen free access to forests will continue. Now, with the declaration of National Parks and Sanctuaries most of the forest areas has been covered under them and restrictions have been imposed on people including the tribesmen to enter into these areas. When the tribes are relocated their accessibility to the medicinal plants is prohibited. Here that by the declaration of protected areas the Government encroaches upon the intellectual property rights of the tribes.

(2) Customary Easements v. Land Acquisition

The Section 2(b) of the Indian Easement Act, 1882 states that nothing herein contained shall be deemed to affect any laws not hereby expressly repealed; or derogate from any customary or other right (not being a license) in or over immovable property which the Government, the public or any person may possess irrespective of other immovable property.

Section 4 of the said Act states that an easement is a right which the owner or occupier of certain land possess, as such, for the beneficial enjoyment of that land, to do and continue to do something, or to prevent and continue to prevent something being done, in or upon, or in respect of, certain other land not his own.

Section 18 of the Easement Act hasprovisions for customary easement, which states that an easement may be acquired in virtue of a local custom. Such easements are called customary easements. For example by the custom of a certain village every cultivator of village land is entitled, as such, to graze his cattle on the common pasture.

In Prabhawati Devi *vs.* Mahendra Singh,[9] : Customary easements, as they are called in section 18 of the Act should be distinguished from the customary rights referred to in section 2(b) of the Act. The latter are rights arising by custom but unappurtenant to a dominant tenement. No fixed period of enjoyment is necessary to establish these rights, but the custom must be reasonable and certain.

As we know that the tribesmen used to reside in the protected area before the declaration of those areas as protected area. They are entitled for customary easements by virtue of being the residents of those areas. The land, now declared as protected area is government land. It has been used as the dominant heritage by the tribesmen from times immemorial. These easements were in the form of grazing their cattles, collection of livestock etc. But after the declaration of these areas as National Park and Sanctuaries under the Wild Life Protection Act, these activities have been restricted and prohibited. It could be observed here that section 35 of Wild Life (Protection) Act and the Indian Easements Act lay stress on two different things at the same time resulting into conflicting provisions.

(3) M.P. Land Revenue Code v. Wild Life (Protection) Act

Section 2 of the M.P. Land Revenue Code, 1959 states that it extends to the whole of M.P. but is not applicable to reserve and protected forests declared under Indian Forest Act, 1927. As Wild Life (Protection) Act has provisions for the declaration of protected areas, i.e. National Park, Sanctuaries, Community reserve and Conserve reserve, there is no specific provision in M.P. Land Revenue Code, 1959 which mentions that whether these protected areas should be included or excluded from the above stated code.

If we presume the inclusion of the protected areas under the M.P. Land Revenue Code, 1959 than, obviously the provision of M.P. Land Revenue Code will be applicable over these areas. But, in such case what will happen to the provision of the Wild Life (Protection) Act, which are in contravention with the provision of the M.P. Land Revenue Code. I feel, that the lawmakers have not dealt with this situation and there still remains ambiguity or legal conflict as to the application of Wild Life (Protection) Act vis-a-vis M.P. Land Revenue Code.

(4) The Panchayat (Extension to Scheduled Areas) Act, 1996 v. Wild Life (Protection) Act

The Panchayat (Extension to the Schedule Areas) Act, 1996, empowers the Gram Sabha and Panchayat to prevent alienation of land in the scheduled areas and to take appropriate action to restore any unlawful alienated land of Scheduled Tribe. This Act also provides that the Gram Sabha or Panchayat shall be consulted before acquiring land in the scheduled areas for various public purpose.

The Wild Life (Protection) Act has mentioned that land can be acquired for protected areas as per the Land Acquisition Act but the incorporation of powers of Gram Sabha and Panchayat has not been mentioned there. It implies that land can be acquired from the tribes even without consultation with the Gram Sabha or the Panchayat.

(iii) Critical Appraisal of Wild Life Laws

During my study I have come across certain provisions, which seems unsatisfactory. There are some provisions, which are either not included in the Act or included with some errors. These are as follows :

(1) *Lacuna in Definitions*

No legal definition has been provided to some important terms in the Wild Life (Protection) Act, 1972. For example, the terms—"Buffer Zone", "Conservation Reserve" and "Community Reserve" have not been defined under the Act.

(2) *Categories of Protected Areas*

Basically, Wild (Protection) Act has 4 categories of protected areas i.e., National Park, Sanctuaries, Conservation Reserve Community Reserve. While the World Conservation Union has an internationally accepted range of different categories of protected areas. Hence it is required to extend some more categories through which traditional, cultural and religious rights should not be ignored and the Government must get fully envisaged with local community and control of management.

(3) *Computation of Compensation*

Whenever land is acquired, compensation is given to the affected person. But no compensation is provided for the land commonly used by the whole community.

(4) *Boundaries are not Clear*

Section 18 does not give any systematic guideline or a clear demarcation of the boundaries for a sanctuary. The main emphasis of administration is towards their own convenience. Even the notifications are not clear with respect to the map of the area or areas declared. Sometimes and they give boundary only the name of the Villages. These errors give birth to boundary disputes.

(5) *Inquiry by Collector*

The Collector shall, after service of the prescribed notice upon the claimant, expeditiously inquire into:

(a) the claim preferred before him clause (b) of section 21 of Wild Life (Protection) Act, 1972;

(b) the existence of any right mentioned in section 19 and not claimed under clause (b) of section 21—so far as the same may be ascertainable from the records of the State

Government and the evidence of any person acquainted with the same.

According to this section Government wants the record of the plot holders which are really very difficult for the tribesmen to produce because of illiteracy and ignorance

(6) Sub Section 3 of Section 35 of the Wild Life (Protection) Act states that where any area is intended to be declared as a National Park, the provisions of Sections 19 to 26A (both inclusive except clause (c) of subsection (2) of Section (24) shall, as far as may be, apply to the investigation and determination of claims, and extinguishment of rights, in relation to any land in such area as they apply to the said matters in relation to any land in a sanctuary.

Section 24 (2)(c) is not applicable in case of National Parks. This means that no habitation can be permitted in National Parks. But reality is contrary to it. There are still eight villages which exist along with other habitation inside the Kanha National Park. Despite so many years non-settlement of case the tribesmen still live in these areas.

Notes and References

1. http://www.cfac.uk/cplan/sacl/cs-indigenous-people.pdf.
2. http://www.cfac.uk/cplan/sacl/cs-indigenous-people.pdf.
3. AIR 1960 SC 932.
4. AIR 1983 SC 109.
5. AIR 1986 SC 180, 193.
6. AIR 1989 SC 549.
7. 1995 Supp (2) SCC 225.
8. 1995 Supp (2) SCC 225.
9. AIR 1981 Pat 133.

Writer with the Tribemen at a Villege Adjacent to the Kanha National Park

5

Conflict between the Wild Life Laws and the Rights of the Tribes in the Protected Areas of Madhya Pradesh

A protection strategy which alienates the local communities is unjust to them and disrespectful of their fundamental rights, as also short-sighted for wild-life conservation. These communities could become the most effective conservationists of natural habitats, as in many cases they have traditionally been if their continued survival is based on these areas and if their immense knowledge about local biodiversity is adequately recognised and harnessed.[1]

Tribal Community as the Protector of Wild Life

The life of tribal people is totally dependent upon forests which is a home for wild animals. The same habitat for two living creatures can be a good reason for conflict between them. Since the habitat for the wild animals and the tribal people is the same, it can become a good reason for conflict between them. But this conflict should not be construed in the sense that the tribal people destroy the life of wild animals for there selfish-interests.

No doubt man is selfish by nature. He can cause any harm to others for his selfish interests. But the tribal society is different from the so-called cultured society which exploits the forests and wild life for luxurious purposes. On the other hand the tribal people are simple living people and if they destroy the forests or kill the wild life than it is only to satisfy the basic necessities of their lives.

Disturbance in ecology is not due to destruction caused by the tribal people but due to unsystematic growth and development, unplanned deforestation and industrialisation, and uncontrolled urbanisation, etc. of the human society.

What we notice in tribal myths and customs and the forests is a situation of mutual dependence. Forest dwellers are totally dependent on forest product's for their basic needs like food, clothing, medicine housing, etc. Their socio-economic life is too much dependent on the forest life. Their customs and culture give importance to animals, fruits and plants. The inter dependence between forests and tribes is so much that separation of either can destroy the originality of the nature itself. And this dependence is not destructive, on the contrary, it is constructive in nature. Tribal people always protect the forest and wild life because their tradition and culture has taught them treat these as "God" who has provided them this life.

Who Wins and Who Loses?

The uncontrolled increase in world population gave birth to rapid deforestation. This invariably resulted in ecological imbalance and the destruction of wild life. How to preserve these became the burning question before man. It resulted in the declaration of reserve forests and protected areas, which were considered as a separate parts of land to protect the forest and wild life.

Comparison of the Western concept with the Indian concept of the "Protected Areas" show that the western concept on protected areas prohibit people from entering these areas whereas due to the habitation of tribes in India the concept of PA changes here.

"A national survey done in the late 1980's in India revealed that 69% of the surveyed PA's had human population (perhaps upwards of 3 million) living inside, and 64% had community rights lease, or concessions inside them."[2]

Therefore in countries like India the Protected Areas are also considered as the home for indigenous community and also the protector of wild life and ecology. This does not mean that there is no need at all to protect the wild life or make laws relating to the protection of wild life. What is required is that the laws should be made on the basis of field study. So that the practical aspects of the areas be taken into consideration. It should be framed in such manner that the rights of indigenous people should not be infringed. Foreign laws cannot be implemented or enforced here because their cultural, ecological, social and economical condition are quite different.

Madhya Pradesh has the highest tribal population in India. Hence, it becomes the responsibility of the State law-makers to make such laws, which should conserve wild life and at the same time protect the rights of the tribal, people here. In Madhya Pradesh Protected Areas are increasing day-by-day. This has given rise to conflicts between the laws relating to wild life and that of the rights of tribal people.

WILD LIFE CONSERVATION IN THE STATE OF MADHYA PRADESH

Madhya Pradesh has a large forest area which contains innumerable species of flora and fauna. Despite the abundance of natural benevolence there are numerous and multifarious problems also, which are faced by the tribes here.

Before we proceed further into the study of this chapter, let us have a glance at the area covered by the forest in Madhya Pradesh.

Forest Area At a Glance:[3]

1. Forest Area—30.89% (95,221.14 sq.km.) of the State's geographical area of 3,08,252 sq.km.
2. Forest Types—Dry thorn to tropical moist deciduous.
3. Reserve Forest—58,733.673 sq.km.
4. Protected Forest—35,586.986 sq.km.
5. Unclassed Forest—900.481 sq.km.
6. Per capita Forest—0.196.
7. Area under JFM—33,85,930 ha.
8. More than 1,000 species of flowering plants including ferns, orchids, medicinal and aromatic plants.

Madhya Pradesh
Wildlife Protected Areas

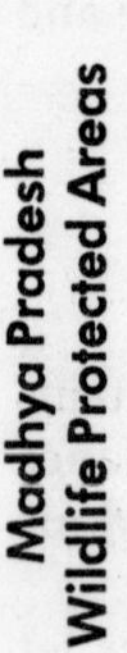

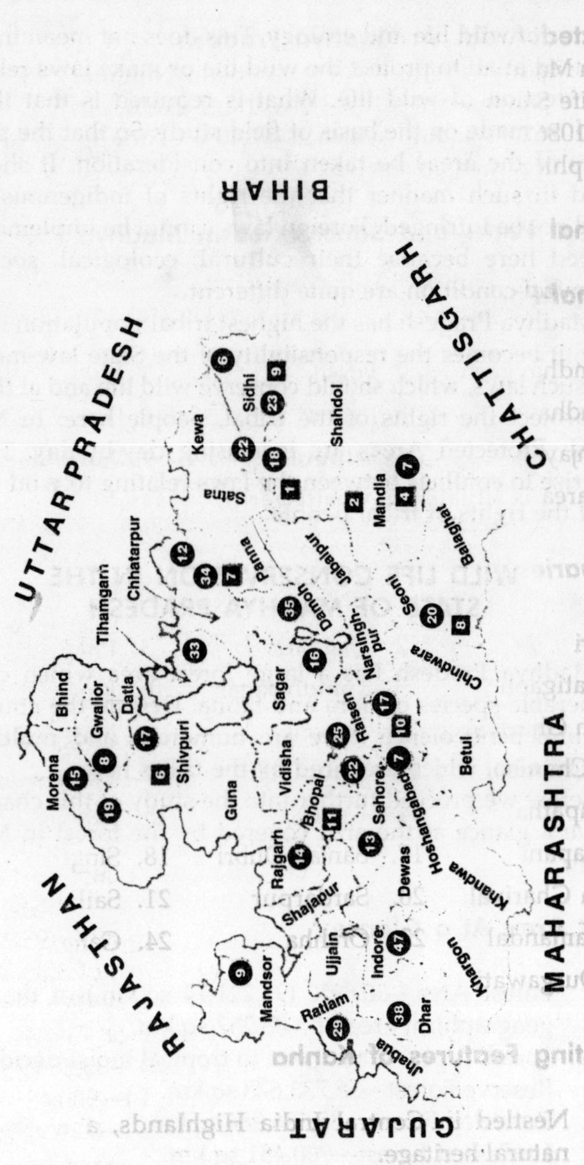

Source: Rajesh, Gopal and Rakesh Shukla ed. *Tiger Conservation Initiatives, Madhya Pradesh "Produce for the M.P."*—Forest Department, 2000, 28.

Protected Areas in Madhya Pradesh

In Madhya Pradesh, there are total 9 National Parks and 25 Wild life Sanctuaries in the network of Protected Areas. These cover 10862.00 sq.km. which is 11.40% of the forest area and geographical area covers 3.52%.

National Parks and Sanctuaries in Madhya Pradesh[4]

National Parks

1. Bandhavgarh	2. Fossil	3. Kanha
4. Madhav	5. Panna	6. Pench
7. Sanjay*	8. Satpura	9. Van Vihar

*(Part area is situated in Chattisgarh).

Sanctuaries

1. Bori	2. Bagdara	3. Phen
4. Ghatigaon	5. Gandhisagar	6. Karera
7. Ken Ghariyal	8. Kheoni	9. Narsinghgarh
10. N. Chambal	11. Nauradehi	12. Pachmari
13. Panpatha	14. Kuno	15. Pench
16. Ratapani	17. Sanjay Dubri	18. Singhori
19. Son Ghariyal	20. Sardarpur	21. Sailana
22. Ralamandal	23. Orchha	24. Gangau
25. V. Durgawati		

Interesting Features of Kanha

(i) Nestled in Central India Highlands, a world-class natural heritage.

(ii) Pride itself on being the first sanctuary of the country since 1935—a long history of conservation.

(iii) Legal status improved and its are consistently increased to the present area of 1838 sq.km. comprising of 940 sq.km. core, a National Park, 898 sq.km. buffer, a "multiple use area".

(iv) Phen Sanctuary in the east, established in 1983 as a satellite mini-core of Kanha. Being developed to provide refuge to migrating wild animals."[5]

Pench, The Timeless Jungle

(i) Constituted in 1992 with a total area of 757.86 sq.km., the core zone (292.85 sq.km.) of the Reserve is a National Park.

(ii) The Pench river flowing south to north virtually divides the park into two. The terrain is generally undulating, forested with tropical moist and dry deciduous teak, and dry mixed deciduous forests.

(iii) Damming of the Pench river creates a hugs 54 sq. km. reservoir in south central part of the park.

(iv) Improved considerably over the years. Currently participatory rural appraisals, microplanning and pilot implementation of ecodevelopment activities under the GEF-India Ecodevelopment Project are under way. [6]

Bandhavgarh, the Wondrous Woods

(i) Of the 1161.471 sq.km. area, 624.752 sq.km. is the core, which includes the National Park.

(ii) A good relative abundance of tigers, and sightings are very common.

(iii) Many hills and hillocks dotting the area amidst valleys meadous, and marshes.

(iv) Forested with tropical dry and moist deciduous forests interspersed with grasslands.

(v) Focus on protection and prevention, besides habitat improvement, ecotourism and ecodevelopment.

(vi) Ecodevelopment inputs under way to elicit the public support.[7]

A Brief Description about Kanha Land

Proposal in the form of the management plan for Kanha Tiger Reserve and Phen Wild Life Sanctuary a Satellite Micro Core of the National Park has been approved by notification of the Government of Madhya Pradesh.

LOCATION

Kanha Tiger Reserve forms part of the Central Indian Highlands spreading across (Madhya Pradesh) from West to East, and is internationally renowned for its anthropological and natural attributes since long.

Falling in the districts of Mandla and Balaghat, the Tiger Reserve lies within the Maikal hills, situated between the Mahadeo hills of Pachmari and Chota Nagpur at the following geographical coordinates.

Longitude = 800-26′-10″ To 810-4′-40″
Latitude = 200-1′-5″ To 220-27′-48″8

CONSTITUTION

The Protected Area is comprised of two divisions, namely the Core Zone (National Park) and the Buffer Zone (Multiple use area). Besides, there is also a Wild life, Sanctuary, namely the Phen, which also serves as a Satellite Micro Core. All these three conservation units are under the unified administration of Kanha Tiger Reserve.

Extent

The area of the Core Zone (National Park) is 940 sq. km. and that of the Buffer Zone is 1009 sq.km. (including several-patches of orange area), adding upto 1949 sq.km. as the total area Kanha Tiger Reserve. The area of Phen Wild life Sanctuary is 110 sq.km[9].

Brief History of Kanha National Park

- The oldest information available on the history of these wilds dates back to around the 19th Century. Kanha Tiger Reserve, forming part of the Gondwana tract was inhabited by two main aboriginal tribes, namely the Gond and the Baiga, both forests dwellers and skilled woodsmen, practising shifting cultivation on all possible topographical features, and exploiting all types of forest produce for their sustenance and livelihood.

- The "Baojar valley", forming the western segment, was declared a Reserve Forest in the year 1879, whereas the reservation in the Halon valley was completed by 1890.
- The earliest account of the faunal glory of this area has been described in Captain J. Forsyth's monumental treatise—"Highlands of Central India" (1989).
- On the 16th of May, 1935, an area of 257 sq. km. of the Banjar valley and about 500 sq.km. of the Halon valley were declared absolute Wild life Sanctuaries, prohibiting all kinds of shooting except that of wild boars and birds.
- The Kanha Sanctuary was notified as a National Park on 01-01-1955, Subsequently, a post of Park Superintendent was created in 1960.
- The initial area of the National Park was 253 sq.km. which with subsequent extensions in 1964 and 1970, assumed a size of 446 sq.km. With the launch of Project Tiger in 1973, the Halon Valley area was eventually integrated with the Kanha National Park, thereby increasing the total area to 940 sq.km., which constitutes the present "Core Zone" area of the Tiger Reserve. The area of the surrounding 'Buffer Zone' amounts to 1009 sq.km. which has been notified by the Govt. as a Separate division with a Drawing and Disbursing Officer (DDO), designated as Dy. Director, Buffer Zone, under the sq. km. unified administrative control of the Chief Conservator Forests and Field Director".[10]

Kanha and the Tribal People

When we talk about the relation and conflicts between the tribal people and Kanha, it is necesary to accept the natural fact that Kanha is not apart from the tribal people much before the declaration of Kanha as a National Park, Kanha was the habitat of these tribal people. Let us read the following lines from Management Plan for Kanha Tiger Reserve.

"The old records indicate that the villagers had free access to cut and burn forests at will. The system of shifting cultivation, locally called the "Bewar", prevailed almost unhindered until as late as 1870 on the hill slopes."[11]

Extraction of forest produce by the villagers under the commutation system for domestic and agricultural use was introduced in 1879 to regulate the unrestricted hacking by villagers. This system also proved quite ineffective and was gradually curtailed, and finally stopped in 1933. Villagers were drawing most of their domestic requirements from the "rayotwari" and the "malguzari" forests, which are not included in the Tiger Reserve. After the abolition of the ex-proprietary rights some supplies of the cut material to meet the "nistar" demands of villagers were permitted from annual coupes under working later, even this was discontinued, and the nistar cut material was made available from special depots opened in the villages.[12]

Field Work at Kanha

On my visit to Kanha National Park situated in Madhya Pradesh, from 6-06-2003 to the 20-06-2003. I had the opportunity to talk and interview a number of tribal people, forest officers, and some local persons.

Firstly, the-tribal people were hesitant and tried to avoid any kind of conversation but after much persuasion, they gradually came out with problems like fuel, shortage of foodgrains and jobs. But the paramount problem they faced was of rehabilitation and relocation and to top it all the avoidance of laws by the forest officers themselves.

When I asked them why did they leave the place, their answer was: "सरकार ने बोला है तो जाना ही पड़ेगा" The tribal people have to abide by the dictates of the forest authorities and if they do not bow down to their commands they have to pay heavily. It shows the deterrent, pathetic condition of these people and how their inherent right to be heard is put away with.

In India the statistics regarding the education of tribal people is very discouraging. Their education level is very low. A survey was conducted to ascertain their education level in selected areas.

From the Table 5.1 one can see that out of 100 respondents, 80 males and 20 females only 5% females are literate as compared to 15% males. In all over 90% of the population is uneducated. 10% belongs to the educated category in which 6.25 is primary

TABLE 5.1
Education of Tribal People

	Male	Female	
Uneducated	68	19	90%
Primary	6	1	6.25%
H.-School	5	—	2.5%
Graduate	1	—	0.5%
Law knowing	—	—	—
Total	80	20	100

school pass, 0.5% is graduate and 2.5% high school Pass. As far as awareness regarding the legal norms about wild life and tribal laws is concerned, they were found absolutely ignorant of the same.

The above scenario clearly indicates the educational status of the tribal people and their knowledge of the tribal laws.

TABLE 5.2
Occupation of Respondents

Occupation Before Relocation	
Labour	2
Collection of Livestock	75
Agriculture	21
Business	2
Service	—
Total	100

As far as occupation of the respondents before relocation is concerned, one can see that 75% of the population was engaged in the collection of livestock for their livelihood 75. Due to higher illiteracy rate business opportunities are negligible i.e. only 2% belonged to the labour class whereas 21% were engaged in agriculture.

The Table 5.3 provides evidence that majority of the tribal people depend on the collection of livestock for their occupation.

TABLE 5.3
Occupation

After Relocation	
Labour	19
Collection of Livestock	18
Agriculture	52
Business	8
Service	3
Total	100

The process of relocation has drastically changed the mode of occupation of the respondents. As is evident from the above table there is tremendous downfall in their traditional occupation of the collection of livestock. From 75% before relocation the percentage goes down to 18% in the after relocation phase. This is a disturbing issue for the tribal people as the relocation process has virtually, snatched their traditional mode of livelihood, there by depriving them of their right to life.

The occupation of agriculture witnesses more then hundred per cent increase in relocation, from 21% it has gone up to 52%. This change is primarily, due to their present condition. The government has provided them with 4.5 acres of land per relocated family for this purpose. The respondents are thus forced to change their occupation and adopt the occupation of agriculture for which they do not have requisite expertise and experience. At the same time the quality of land allotted to them is barren in most of the cases. Therefore the adoption of agriculture as their occupation is of little benefit to them.

In the relocated group we find the emergence of the service class also which is a positive sign. 3% of the population has gone for the of service. Business class has also witnessed an increase from 2% to 8% in the relocated group.

Thus one can see that the tribal people are forced to adopt new modes of occupation without being provided the technical and other required expertise of it.

TABLE 5.4
Response to Relocation

Agriculture	*Unsatisfied*	*Satisfied No.*	*Response*	*Total*
Below 20 yrs.	24	14	1	39
21-40	11	15	—	26
41-60	8	10	4	22
Above 60	9	2	2	13
Total	52	41	07	100

Effect of Relocation

The study posed a question to the respondents regarding their opinion about relocation, that is, whether they were satisfied with their present status after relocation. 57.6% of the population falling within the age group of 21-40 years and 45.4% of the population falling within the age group of 41-60 years is satisfied after the relocation whereas 42.3% of the population in the age group of 21-40 years and 36.3% of the population in the age group of 41-60 years is not satisfied. But the situation surprisingly changes when one goes below 20 years where 61.5% of the population is not satisfied and only 35.8% is satisfied. Again considering the population of the age group above 60 years one notices that 69.2% of the population is not satisfied and only 15.3% of the population is satisfied. Leaving the age group aside, if one calculates the overall percentage of satisfied population, it comes to about 38.5% approximately and the overall percentage of unsatisfied population comes to about 52.3% approximately.

The reason for increased percentage of unsatisfied people above 60 years after relocation can be said to be due to the long years of their stay at the protected areas. Naturally, they must have developed emotional and psychological bonds with their previous places and environment. Since the elder ones had spent maximum part of their life in their previous habitat it must have been difficult for them to readjust with the new surroundings. On the other hand as the younger generation has the capacity to adjust itself to the changing circumstances, the percentage of its population increases towards the satisfied group.

TABLE 5.5
Declaration of Protected Areas

Age	*Satisfied With Present*	*Not Satisfied/ Prefer*	*Total Changes*
Below 20 yrs.	9	30	39
21-40	7	10	26
41-60	3	19	22
61 and above	4	9	13
Total	23	77	100

Views of the respondents regarding the process of Declaration of Protected Areas

The survey also enquired about the views of the respondents regarding the prevalent process of declaration of Protected areas. As is evident from the above table majority of them, i.e., 77%, are not satisfied with the present process of declaration. Only 23% have registered their satisfaction.

Another supplementary question was asked to respondents who were not satisfied with the above process. It was with respect to the changes they would prefer in the existing system. Of the 77% who had shown their preference for changes, all were in favour of complete settlement of their rights before the declaration. The reason for this change was because of the poor stand of the Government in most of the cases where settlement of rights was done after the declaration. Thus a sense of betrayal was witnessed widespread amongst the respondents and they wanted that the settlement should be done prior to declaration.

The respondents were further enquired about their disputes with the forest officials. Substantial number of respondents, i.e. 67% admitted the existence of disputes with the forest officials. Only 33% admitted harmonious relations with the forest officials.

Table 5.6
Disputes with the Forest Officials

Sl. No.	*Response*	*No. Response*
1.	Disputes Exist	67
2.	Disputes do not Exist	33
	Total	100

Table 5.7
Nature of Disputes

	Nature	*No.*
1.	Animals Entry	13
2.	Relocation Problems	23
3.	Livestock Collection	19
4.	Allegation of Official	5
5.	Others	7
	Total	67

The respondents who admitted about the existence of disputes had various reasons for 19.4% admitted their dispute due to their animals entry into the protected areas. Many a times their animals strayed into the limits of the protected areas for grazing purpose. The problem before them arises as to how to bring them back as in order to bring them back they themselves have to enter into the area of protected forest and such an entry is also considered as a crime by the forest officials. The moment these people move towards the forest they are apprehended by the officials. 34.35% stated that the relocation process was a cause of dispute for them. These respondents disagree to the process of relation. 28.3% held the collection of livestock responsible for the dispute. The tribal people enter the restricted areas so as to collect their life supporting materials, and this entrance brings them into direct conflict with the forest officials. As a consequence, they get arrested for violating the laws.

TABLE 5.8
Resolving the Disputes

S.N.	*Institution*	*No.*
1.	Courts	9
2.	Panchayats	18
3.	Mutual Settlement	40
	Total	67

As is clear from the above table that 59.7% of the concerned population prefer to use the mutual settlement process for resolving their disputes. These people are apprehensive about the legal and constitutional machinery. It may be attributed to be due to their lack of education awareness and information. The respondents who admitted that they had gone to the court confessed that they did not approach it on their own free will, rather they had to go there because the officials had filed petition against them for the so-called offences. 26.8% respondents preferred going to the panchayats. This reflects their confidence in the third tier of Indian democracy, i.e., the panchayats.

Another side of the Horizon

Problems faced by the Forest Officers are as follows:

1. Government enforces laws on the tribal areas and accordingly the forest officers have to deal with it. Some forest officers, were also interviewed. They said that they have to face problems when the law of relocation is imposed on the tribal persons. The Tribal people who are satisfied with the implementation of laws of wild life are not so difficult to be handled but those who are unwilling to leave their places are the really troublesome ones. The situation becomes worse when these tribal people start agitating and form a mob. It is the forest officers who had to face such mobs and diffuse tension so as to ascertain that the rule of law is enforced.

2. Another problem is the problem of licence. The Government has given guns or pistols to the Range Officers or forest officers but they are not suppose to use it because it was not licensed.
3. Another problem arose out of the indirect indulgence of local and forest officers. The indulgence should be direct so that the problem of tribal people can be solved quickly. In 2001 Eco-development committees were formed in which local and forest officers and the Government was involved. Similarly amendment should to made so that the local or Forest Officers could be involved directly.

Notes and References

1. Ashish Kothari, "Is Joint Management of Protected Areas Desirable and Possible?," ed. Ashish Kothari, *et. al.*, *People and Protected Area,* (New Delhi: Sage Publication, 1996) 18.
2. Saloni Suri, "People's Involvement in Protected Areas Experiences from Abroad and Lessons for India," (New Delhi, Sage Publication, 1996) 248.
3. Rajesh, Gopal and Rakesh Shukla ed., *Tiger Conservation Initiatives, Madhya Pradesh* "Produce for the M.P.", Forest Department, 2000, 12.
4. Rajesh Gopal and Rakesh Shukla, 12.
5. Rajesh Gopal and Rakesh Shukla, 18.
6. Rajesh Gopal and Rakesh Shukla, 23.
7. Rajesh Gopal and Rakesh Shukla, 25.
8. Rajesh Gopal and Rakesh Shukla, Management Plan for Kanha Tiger Reserve. For the Period 2001-2002 to 2010-2011, 2000, 3.
9. Gopal, Rajesh and Rakesh Shukla, 3.
10. Gopal, Rajesh and Rakesh Shukla, 26 and 27.
11. Gopal, Rajesh and Rakesh Shukla, 28.
12. Gopal, Rajesh and Rakesh Shukla, 28.

6

Judicial Trends

We have discussed the relevant laws and the problems related to wild life and the tribes. In this chapter we shall discuss another important aspect of the subject which pertains to the judicial pronouncements. Judiciary, as we know, is not only the interpreter of law: statutory, constitutional, customary, or otherwise, but also the creator of it.

> It has, therefore, intervened to protect democracy and the rule of law on which the Constitution rests. The Court has always been guided by the Latin maxim *boni judicis est ampliare jurisdictionem*, that law must keep pace with society to retain its relevance, for if the society moves but law remains static, it shall be bad for both. In order to create a civil society in which respect for human dignity is the corner-stone of it's functioning, the Supreme Court has zealously protected the human rights of individuals.[1]

The achievements of Supreme Court have been significant in all areas of the nation's life. It has decided cases touching all facets of human life.

Today, it is because of public opinion that the higher

judiciary in the country occupies a position of pre-eminence among the three organs of the State. An independent judiciary is a national asset.[2]

Judiciary being a defender of Constitution and guardian of Human Rights has played a vital role to make a balanced society and specially maintain equality amongst its polity.

The Court has always been aware of its special responsibility towards the weaker sections of the society, who due to poverty, ignorance, and illiteracy find it difficult to access the Court for justice. Hence, it evolved the strategy of public interest litigation (or social action litigation) to bring justice within the reach of the underprivileged classes. PIL has evolved as an effective tool of the justice delivery system, wehre the traditional concept of *locus standi* has been expanded. PIL has led to many landmark judgement and is the tool that has helped the Court to act its role of the social engineer.[3]

This shows the positive approach of Supreme Court of India towards weaker section of the society or the tribesmen.

In the last fifty years, the apex court has acted as the protector, guardian and interpreter of fundamental rights and has sought to integrate them with directive principles.[4]

The true nature of laws can only be understood by going through the judgements of the courts. Our legal conclusions and solutions remain Half-baked until views of the courts are taken into account. This thesis will remain incomplete unless it includes the view of the judiciary as expressed in their judgements. In this chapter, therefore, we are going to analyse some of the important court cases on the subject. However, instead of just reporting the decisions and their meanings, what we intend to do is to try to discuss a trend from those judgements. It will be our endeavour, therefore, in this chapter, to present a cogent judicial trend on the subject.

Now the battles are drawn between the protectors of wild life, on one side, and the protectors of the affected tribal communities on the other. The controversy is that while the former say that National Parks and Sanctuaries protect the ecological balance and preserve the forests, the latter say that the decision adversely affects the rights of the tribes and that it is wrong to say that tribes kill animals for profit. Of course, sometimes there may be a need to kill, either to protect their life when they are attacked or for food when there is nothing else to eat. But such occasions are rare and such actions, under the circumstances, are permitted in all societies and almost in all religions.

Ultimately this battle rests upon the Supreme Court to solve the problems of conflicting interests and it has been trying to achieve a balance between the two, as is evident from the following cases enumerated. Let us consider if there is any trend which is discernible.

Banwasi Sewa Ashram *v.* State of U.P.[5] The Supreme Court directed the Record Officer and Forest Settlement Officer to relax the procedural rigor of Section 4 and Section 6 of the Forest Act and adopt a suitable procedure that would adequately safeguard the rights, interests of the *Adivasis* and it *Banwasis* living in Mirzapur district of U.P. before constituting reserve forest there.

Although it is a case which talks about the procedural rigor of Indian Forest Act and its impact on tribesmen of a particular area, but at the same time directs that procedure can be changed to provide Justice to the tribesmen. This should be I applicable to the protected areas declared under Wild Life (Protection) Act, 1972 and the rights of the tribes can be safeguarded. Thus in my opinion this is a vital judgement which favours the tribal people's interests.

Niyamavedi v. State of Kerala and etc.[6]

Petitioner 'Niyamavedi, Kalvathy, Kochi' has filed this petition challenging the action of the first respondent to establish a Biological Park in 'Agasthyavanam'. This Petition has been filed as a public interest litigation.

Petitioners contended that the proposed project for Biological Park would result in denudation of forest in the State of Kerala, that it would amount to violation of Forest Conservation Act that Central Government's consent has not been obtained for the project and if the project materialises it would pose threat to the environment and ecology. It was contended by them that the forest wealth in the State is considerably depleted on account of the callous attitude of the Government and as there is likelihood of thousands of valuable trees being cut and removed under the guise of the project, prompt judicial action is called for.

Petitioners have a further contention that there are six Adivasi settlements having ancient civilisation in the Agasthyavanam and if the Biological Park becomes a fait accomplish it would virtually result in their ouster from their abodes.

Construction of buildings in the Neyyar Wild Life Sanctuary is challenged by the petitioners on the ground that such construction would destroy the Agasthyamala and its environment. Petitioner contend that construction of buildings is in violation of the provisions of the Forest Conservation Act and that the diversion of the forest area for non-forest purpose is illegal. Petitioners also attacked the project report on the ground that no steps are taken to accommodate the tribals, that the establishment of the Biological Park is against the directions issued by this Court is O.P. 4084 of 1986 and that the construction of administrative block, staff quarters and residential buildings for the tourists contravenes the Forest Conservation Act. It is asserted in O.P. 9741/1992 that places where quarters are proposed to be constructed are inside of Neyyar Sanctuary area which is within the proposed Agasthyamala biosphere reserve.

Additional Advocate General submitted that the petitioners are under a mistaken impression that the establishment of Biological Park would be detrimental to the ecological system in the country and that it infringes the Forest Conservation Act, the directions issued by this Court in O.P. 4084 of 1986 and Wild Life (Protection) Act. It is contended by him that the prima purpose of the project is really afforestation and protection of the forest. It is asserted that no tree would be cut and removed unnecessarily and the apprehension that the forest wealth will be destroyed is without any basis. This is a project approved by the State Planning Board, Planning Commission of India and included in the 8th Five Year Plan. Major portion of the area where the Biological Park is sought to be established is a degraded forest and at present this is a heaven for boot-legers and anti-social elements.

It can be seen that the State Government constituted a Scientific Committee in 1992 and requested the Committee to scrutinise the preliminary project report of the proposed project and to assess its technical viability and the Committee made a threadbare study about it and gave it a final shape.

Stand of the first respondent is that the area is highly degraded forest and that it has all the potentials for bio-conservation and development. The essential idea of the project is conservation of the flora and fauna of the Western Ghats of Kerala and that if the proposal as envisaged in the report is implemented the area can be developed into a model Biological Park. Out of the 23 Sq. Kms. area earmarked for the park, about 17.5 Sq.kms. will be set apart for natural regeneration.

The allegation that large number of concrete buildings would be put up inside the wild forest is emphatically denied by the first respondent. It is stated in the counter affidavit that most of the buildings required for the project area proposed to be constructed will be outside the forest area and also in the private land specifically acquired for that purpose.

The allegation that large number of valuable trees will be cut and removed is also denied by the first respondent.

Construction of roads is permitted even under the Wild Life (Protection) Act. Section 33(a) provides that the Chief Wild Life Warden shall be the authority who shall control, manage and maintain all sanctuaries and for that purpose, within the limits of any sanctuary may construct such roads, bridges, buildings, fences or barrier gates and carry out such other works as he may consider necessary for the purpose of such sanctuary. So, the petitioners cannot object to the formation of the road through the project area invoking the provisions under the Wild Life (Protection) Act. Construction of roads would be really necessary for the protection of the Biological Park. For roads only a small portion of the area will be utilised and under no circumstances roads will be constructed through the thick forest area. The existence of road is very essential for the upkeep of the Biological Park and in a case where few trees are cut from the area through which a road passes one cannot jump to the conclusions that as a result of the project, forest has been plundered.

Two things emerge. One is the decision to establish Biological Park. This is an administrative policy decision. Secondly, by establishing Biological Park there is no violation of any statutory or constitutional provision. If there is no such violation, administrative or policy decision cannot be interfered under Article 226 of the Constitution of India.

The State Government has decided to establish Biological Park taking into account the expert opinion and after due deliberations. So long as there is no violation of any statutory provision the policy decision of the Government cannot be interfered by this Court under Article 226 of the Constitution of India.

As the State Government on a consideration of the opinion of the experts and scientists have decided that the establishment of the Biological Park would really be conducive to the proper maintenance of the forest wealth and as it is a badly needed step for afforestation this Court cannot intervene in matter which is completely within the executive powers of the Government and which is purely administrative in nature especially when there is no evidence of any patent abuse of power.

The relief prayed for in the Original Petitions cannot be allowed. Original Petitions are dismissed.

In this case the petitioners have contended that there are six Adiwasi settlements having ancient civilization in the Agasthavana and if the biological park becomes a fait accomplish it would virtually result in their ouster from the abodes and no steps are taken to accommodate the tribesmen.

I have not come across any comment by the Hon'ble Court on this contention although the court held that acquisition of land for the establishment of biological park is valid and it is an administrative decision in which Court cannot interfere. It shows that the property rights of the tribesmen were it not properly considered by the Court and displacement of the tribes from their ancestral habitations is not treated as a violation of constitutional as well as statutory right of the tribes and at the same time the Court has validated the action taken by the executive even after the contention that tribesmen were not accommodated properly.

One can say that the Court cannot deviate from its duty that it has a purely administrative function at the same time the reasonableness of the action should have been put to test and the guidance for accommodation of the displaced tribal people should have been directed.

In case of Tarun Bharat Sungh Alwar v. Union of India and Others[7]

Tarun Bharat Sungh, a voluntary Organisation interested *inter alia* in protection of environment, approached the Court complaining that widespread illegal mining activity was going on in the area declared as Tiger Reserve in Alwar district of Rajasthan. In the interest of ecology, environment and rule of law, it said, the mining activity should be stopped.

After issuing notices to the Government of Rajasthan and the mine-owners the Court gave certain directions on October 11, 1991. An interlocutory direction was issued to the effect that "no mining operation of whatever nature shall be carried on in the protected area".

Petitioner's case was that no mining lease/licence can be granted within the protected forest except with the prior permission of the Government of India and that no such permission was obtained infact.

An affidavit sworn by Shri S.P. Singh, Deputy Director in the Ministry of Environment and Forest, Project Tiger, New Delhi has been filed. It is submitted that the Forest (Conservation) Act applies not only to reserve and protected forest but to all areas recorded as forest in Government records. Mining is non-forestry activity and, therefore, cannot be carried on in the areas to which Forest (Conservation) Act applies without the prior approval of the Government of India. It is stated further that on May 7, 1992, the Government of India has issued the final notification under Section 3 of the Environment (Protection) Act, 1986 prohibiting all mining activity, except with the approval of the Government of India, in the protected forest, Sariska National Park and certain areas of Alwar District mentioned in the notification. Since no permission is obtained under any of the said enactments with respect to the said 262 mines, it is submitted no mining operations can be carried on in the area until and unless they obtain the permission of the Central Government. Indeed, the prohibition extends not merely to protected forest areas but to the entire area declared as Tiger Reserve and as Sariska National Park.

Learned counsel for the State of Rajasthan submitted that the Rajasthan Government and its officers were not aware, when they granted leases/licences in respect of listed mines and that they fell within the area declared as protected forest. Indeed, a certificate was issued by the Forest Department to the effect that they did not fall within the protected forest area. It was thus a bonafide grant. The boundaries of the areas declared as protected areas were not clearly known nor were they demarcated on the spot. On this point the Court has not given any directions.

The petitioner filed a suit to prohibit any type of mining activity because that has already been prohibited by the forest laws of Rajasthan. It was held by the Court that there can be no mining activity in the protected forest area without the prior permission of the Central Govt. Here Court will permit mining operation only after prior permission from the authority. It means that the court is in favour of economic development as well as maintaining ecological balance.

This case throws light on the ecological and economic aspect. No where the rights of the tribes have been discussed in this case. But by this case I have tried to highlight one very important submission which was argued by learned counsel for the State of Rajasthan that "The boundaires of the areas declared as protected areas were not clearly known nor were they demarked on the spot."

On that basis the Government justify its act of issuing certificate to the mine owners. One can understand that due to improper demarcation this mistake is quite obvious. If we see it on the other side that if any person or tribe can enter in a protected area in the mis-conception that it is not a protected area, he commits a crime for which lie can be punished. This shows that it is very difficult for the general public to recognise the boundaries of National Parks and Sanctuaries.

Pradeep Krishan v. Union of India[8]

The petitioner an environmentalist, actuated by public interest, has filed this petition under Article 32 of the Constitution of India challenging the legality and constitutional validity of an order issued by the State of Madhya Pradesh, Department of Forest, No. F. 4/154/91/10/2 dated 28.3.1995, permitting collection of tendu leaves from Sanctuaries and National Parks by villagers living around the boundaries thereof with the avowed object of maintenance of their traditional rights. The petitioner contends that this act of the state Government is *ultra vires* the provisions of the Wild Life (Protection) Act, 1972, as well as the petitioner's fundamental rights guaranteed by Articles 14 and 21 of the Constitution and is even otherwise inconsistent with the Directive Principle contained in Article 48-A and the Fundamental Duty cast on every citizen under clause (g) of the Article 51-A of the Constitution of India. The petitioner further contends that the said order is malafide and against public interest.

The petitioner has, therefore, filed this petition with a view to preserving the ecology, environment and wild life in the National Parks and Sanctuaries which are likely to be adversely affected by the implementation of the impugned order. On the above pleadings and contentions, the petitioner has raised two contentions which have been formulated as under:

(i) Whether an area declared as a Sanctuary and National Park under Section 18 and Section and 35, respectively, of the Wild Life (Protection) Act, 1972 can be exploited for the collection of minor forest produce in violation of the restrictions contained in the said Act ?

and

(ii) Whether the State Government has the right to exploit minor forest produce from the Sanctuaries and National Parks which have been so declared for the protection and preservation of ecology, flora, fauna and geomorphologic, natural or zoological significance ?

Chief Conservator of Forest (Production), Government of Madhya Pradesh, has filed a counter-affidavit contending that since no fundamental right of the petitioner has been violated the petition is not maintainable under Article 32 of the the Constitution. So also, the petitioner has no *locus standi* to challenge the impugned order on the strength of Articles 14, 21 48-A and/or 51 -A(g) of the Constitution of India. The deponent further contends that the traditional rights of the villagers living in and around the boundaries of the National Parks and Sanctuaries in respect of which the final notification under Sections 26-A and 35 of the Wild Life Protection Act, 1972 has not been issued cannot be questioned till the same has been acquired, due compensation has been paid and the villagers have been rehabilitated. He has further contended that the State Government has the right to exploit minor forest produce under the Act. While conceding that the State Government had by its under Article order dated 16.9.1982, forbidden collection of minor forest produce from the Sanctuaries in the year 1982-83, it did permit collection of certain minor forest produce like honey, tamarind, of the mango, mahul leaves, mahul flowers etc. by the tribals for their bonafide use. By order dated 1.9.1983, and by subsequent order dated 7.5.1990, it also permitted collection of tendu leave deponent etc., from the Sanctuaries. The collection was then done departmentally. Again by the order dated 16.4.1992, the State Government permitted collection of forest produce from Sanctuary areas and proposed National Parks departmentally, or through agents, and the local people were permitted to called non-nationalised forest produce for their bonafide use and for sale in the local market. The above orders were partly modified by the order of 13.12.1994 whereby the collection of tendu leaves was permitted to villagers living in an around the areas not notified as Sanctuaries and National Parks under Section 26-A and 35 of the Act.

Dealing with the petitioner's contention regarding the depletion of the forest area, figures have been quoted from the Forest Survey of India showing a gradual improvement in the forest from 1987 to 1991 with a marginal decrease between 1991 ana 1993. However, the petitioner's broad contention in regard to the depletion of the forest cover in the State of Madhya Pradesh remains unassailed.

The deponent further states that there are 11 National Parks and 33 Sanctuaries in the State of Madhya Pradesh, out of which 3 National Parks are finally notified under the National Park Act, 1955 and one Sanctuary is notified under the Act as amended in 1991, but the final notification is yet to be issued. The remaining 8 National Parks and 32 Sanctuaries were notified from time to time under the Act prior to its amendment in 1991. In these

National Parks and Sanctuaries, proceeding under Sections 19 to 25 of the Act were not undertaken in acquiring the rights of the people. That is why they were not finally notified. The State Government could not have taken away the rights of the tribals and villager dependent on minor forest produce without acquisition of those rights after payment of compensation. It is for this reason that the final notification under Section 26-A could not be issued unless provision for payment of compensation and rehabilitation for the same were simultaneously made. So also, in regard to the National Parks, the final declaration could not be issued under Section 35 of the Act for the same reason.

Now, it is very much clear that this, petition is based on misconceived apprehension and suspicion.

Petitioner clarified his stand by saying that we are not challenging the right of the tribes living in and National Parks and the Sanctuaries to collect minor forest produce for their personal bonafide purpose. While my emphasis is only towards the commercial exploitation specially the tendu leaves through contractors, which is not consistent for with the aim and object of the Act.

According to the petitioner, Sanctuaries which were declared sanctuaries even after the amendment in the Act continue as such even after the amendment and their status does not get affected by the amendment and therefore, in respect thereof, a second notification under Section 26A is unnecessary and non-issuance of a fresh notification can't take way the protection extended by Sec. 27 to 34 of the Act.

In the present proceeding, 3 persons (i)- Bali Ram, (ii) Shyam Lal and (iii) Munshilal have filed an application for seeking permission to intervene. According to them, what they the earn from the tendu leaves is barely enough for their sustenance Sanctuaries and is not a big commercial venture as is sought to be made out by the petitioner. They lastly contended that they have been enjoying this privilege for generations and the denial of this privilege to the small tribal population, since their survival is on minor forest produce only, would result in ruination of the entire tribal population.

They therefore contended that no fundamental right of the petitioner, for the matter of environmentalists is violated and the court should refuse to entertain the petition.

Two reliefs are claimed in this writ petition, namely, (i) to quash the notification dated 28.3.1995 issued by the Government of Madhya Pradesh; and (ii) to direct the State Government to strictly enforce the provisions of Sections 27 to 33 of the Act in relation to National Parks and Sanctuaries notified under Sections 18 and 35 of the Act. As pointed out noti earlier, in the rejoinder-affidavit filed by the petitioner, he stated in no uncertain terms that he was not questioning the right of the villagers (tribals) living in and around the National Parks and Sanctuaries to collect minor forest produce therefrom for their personal bonafide use but questions the Government's right to permit commercial exploitation of such produce. That would mean the petitioner does not object to the entry of villagers in the National Parks and Sanctuaries for the limited purpose of collecting the minor forest produce including tendu leaves. If that be so, the apprehension that their entry into those areas would be the cause for fire must recede in the background. Instances of forest fires in Panna National Park and Udayanti Sanctuary were relied on, but there is no material on record to show that these fires were caused by the villagers/tribals who entered the forest to collect minor forest produce.

It is further stated that since 1989, the practice of setting fire to tendu bushes has been completely and totally stopped. Therefore, in the absence of any reliable evidence in that behalf, the apprehension must be stated to be rejected. Even otherwise, in the counter affidavit filed by the State Government, it has been clarified that every precaution has been taken to ensure that no such tragedy takes place and proper arrangements have been made so that there is no danger to the flora and fauna and wild life in those areas. Therefore, we must allow the matter to rest at that.

These allegations have been specifically denied in the State's counter-affidavit. Referring to the Forest Survey of India for 1987 to 1993, it is shown that the actual forest cover has increased and not decreased, the small reduction from 1991 to 1993 is due to interpretational correction and the actual depletion can be said to be only 145 sq.kms. according to the State Government.

It is evident from the above pleading that since neither the traditional rights of those living in the vicinity of these parks and sanctuaries have been acquired, nor have provisions been made to either compensate or rehabilitate them, the final declaration under Sections 26-A and 35 has not been possible. That is the reason why the State Government had to permit collection of tendu leaves by the impugned notification dated correction 28.3.1995.

It is, therefore, not possible to conclude that the State the Government had violated any provision of law in issuing the India and notification dated 28.3.1995 in question.

The matter, however does not rest there. The petitioner contends that the forest cover in the State of Madhya Pradesh gradually shrinking. As pointed out earlier, there is shrinkage to the extent of 145 sq.kms. between 1991 and 1993. In our country, the total forest cover is far less than the ideal minimum of one-third of the total land. We cannot, therefore, afford any further shrinkage in the forest cover in our country. If one of the reasons for this shrinkage is the entry of villagers and tribes living in and around the Sanctuaries and the National Parks, there can be no doubt that urgent steps must be taken to prevent any destruction or damage to the environment, the flora and fauna and wild life in those areas. If the only reason which compels the State Government to permit entry and collection of tendu leaves is not having acquired the rights of villagers/tribes and having failed to locate any area for their rehabilitation, we think that inertia in this behalf cannot be tolerated. We are, therefore, of the opinion that while we do not quash the order of 28.3.1995, we think that the State Government must be directed to decide on the question of completing the process for issuing final notifications and then take urgent steps to complete the procedure for declaring notifying the areas as Sanctuaries and National Parks under Sections 26-A and 35 of the Act. We therefore, direct that the State Government shall take immediate action under Chapter IV of the Act an institute an inquiry, acquire the rights of those who claim any right in or over any land proposed to be included in the Sanctuary/National Park and thereafter proceed to issue a final notification under Section 26-A and 35 of the Act declaring such areas as Sanctuaries/National Park. We direct the State Government to initiate action in this behalf within a period of 6 months from today and expeditiously conclude the same showing that sense of urgency as is expected of a State Government in such matters as enjoined by Article 48-A of the Constitution and at the same time keeping in view the duty enshrined in Article 51-A(g) of the Constitution. We are sure, and we have no reason to doubt, that the State Government would show the required zeal to expeditiously declare and notify the areas as Sanctuaries/National Parks.

The Court rejected the petitioner's apprehension in respect of forest fires.

This is a case where petitioner has challenged the Notification of Government of Madhya Pradesh by which Government has permitted collection of minor forest produce from the National Park by the villagers, but after the respondents plea the petitioner has contended that they were not questioning the rights of the villagers (tribes) living in and around the National Parks and Sanctuaries to collect minor forest produce therefrom for there personal bonafide use, but questions the Government's right to permit commercial exploitation of such produce. This shows that the right to livelihood of the tribes have been recognised by the petitioner also and State Government also contended that the forest cover during 1987 to 1993 has increased and not decreased and neither the traditional right of the people those living in the vicinity of these parks and sanctuaries have been acquired, nor have provisions been made to either compensate or rehabilitate. This is a good decision of the Government of Madhya Pradesh.

In this judgement court has tried to maintain harmonious balance between the ecology and the right of the tribes. Court has directed that as early as possible rights of the tribes should be resettled and until and unless adequate compensation will not be given the rights of the tribes can be continued in the National Parks and Sanctuaries this shows the practical approach of Apex Court.

Animal and Environment Legal Defence Fund *Vs.* Union of India and others[9]

The petitioner is an association of lawyers and other persons who are concerned with the protection of the environment. They have filed the present petition in public interest challenging the order of the Chief Wild Life Warden. Forest Department, Government of Madhya Pradesh (second respondent) granting 305 fishing permits to the tribals formerly residing within the Pench National Park area for fishing in the

Totladoh reservoir situated in the heart of the Pench National Park Tiger Reserve.

The Pench National Park covers an area falling in the States of Madhya Pradesh and Maharashtra. The area which falls in the State of Madhya Pradesh covers two districts, Seoni and Chhindwara. The districts of Seoni and Chhindwara were originally parts of the old C.P. and Berar Province. This area was originally declared as Reserved Forest under the India Forest Act of 1878. It continued to remain as Reserved Forest under the Indian Forest Act of 1927. Under Section 5 of the Indian Forest Act of 1927, once a notification is issued declaring any land as reserved forest no right shall be acquired in or over such land, except by succession or under a grant or contract in writing made or entered into by or on behalf of the Government or some person in whom such right was vested when the notification was issued. Under Section 26(l)(i) of the Indian Forest Act, 1927, any person who in contravention of any rules made in this behalf by the State Government hunts, shoots, fishes, poisons water or sets traps or snares, shall be punishable in the manner provided in that Section. According to the petitioner, in view of these provisions, the ancestors of the present tribals could not have acquired any fishing right in the Pench river. The present permits which are issued in lieu of this traditional right, therefore are unwarranted and must be cancelled or set aside.

Accordingly, by Notification No. 5/15/82-10/77 dated 1.3.1983 the Government, of Madhya Pradesh, Forest Department declared its intention under Section 35(l) of the Wild Life (Protection) Act, 1972, to constitute the areas specified therein as a National Park. The area of Pench National Park so notified was within the two districts of Seoni and Chhindwara. On such declaration, the Collector of the district concerned is required under Section 19 of the Wild Life (Protection) Act, 1972 to enquire into and determine the existence, nature and extent of the rights of any person in or over the land comprised within the limits of the sanctuary.

Under Section 21, the Collector is required to publish in every town and village or in the neighbourhood of the area concerned, a proclamation specifying the situation and the limits of the National Park and requiring any person, claiming any right mentioned in Section 19, to prefer before the Collector, within two months a written claim in the prescribed form specifying the nature and extent of such right with necessary details and the amount and particulars of compensation, if any, claimed in respect thereof.

Under Section 22, the Collector is required to hold an enquiry in the manner specified there. Accordingly on 10.12.1985, the Collector Seoni issued, a proclamation under Sections 19 and 21 inviting claims within 60 days in respect of the areas notified under Section 35(l) by the notification of 1.3.1983. Apparently no one lodged any claim. The Collector issued a final order under Section 24 of the Wild Life (Protection) Act on 28.8.1986.

The Collector Chhindwara similarly issued a proclamation under Sections 19 and 21 inviting claims. As no claims were received, a final order under Section 24 was issued by the Collector of Chhindwara on 27.12.1986. However, notification under Section 35(4) has yet been issued by the Government of Madhya Pradesh declaring the said area as a National Park.

As per the counter-affidavit filed on behalf of the second respondent it has been stated that although the necessary proclamations were issued earlier nobody came forward to claim their rights on account of illiteracy and unawareness.

However, recently three applications regarding claims had been received pertaining to the traditional rights of villagers residing in eight villages within the notified area which have now been relocated outside the National Park area. These villagers are tribal. The villagers claim that they had a traditional right of fishing for their livelihood in the Pench river. They have claimed that their traditional right of fishing should be preserved as this is their only source of livelihood. Most of these tribals have been displaced from their original villages and have been resettled in villages outside the National Park area. Under an order dated 30.5.1996 these tribals have now been given permits to fish in the Totladoh reservoir which came into existence in 1986-87 on construction of a dam across Pench river as a part of the Pench Hydro Electric Project. The reservoir is in the centre of the National Park area which partly falls in Maharashtra and partly in Madhya Pradesh. Apparently, fishing activity has been started in this reservoir by Fisheries Development Corporation of the State of Madhya Pradesh despite protests from the Forest Department.

The petitioner as well as the State of Maharashtra have pointed out that if fishing is permitted in the heart of the National

Park and as many as 305 fishing permits are issued, the biodiversity and ecology of the area will be seriously affected. Fishing activity is a potential source of danger to the National Park because it may also lead to illegal felling of trees or poaching. It will be humanly impossible to monitor licensees, their ingress and agress and to ensure that these licensees do not indulge in poaching and other ecologically harmful activities.

The Collector of Chhindwara in his letter of 7.6.1996 addressed to the Secretary, Government of Madhya Pradesh, Forest Department, in connection with the issuing of a final notification for the establishment of Pench National Park stated that displaced persons from 4 villages namely, Palaspani, Umarighat, Chhindewani and Chhedia have traditional fishing rights in Pench river. After displacement these persons have not been rehabilitated systematically. No agriculture land has been made available to them, no work has been made available to them and they do not have any mean of livelihood except catching fish which is their traditional occupation. If they are not given fishing permission a serious problem of feeding and supporting their families will arise. He has, therefore recommended recognition of traditional rights of 332 families of 4 villages. In view of these reports the State Government has stated on affidavit that it was satisfied that the traditional rights of fishermen had not been settled and instructions were given to the Chief Wild Life Warden for issuing permission for fishing to 305 local fishermen whose names are set out in the annexure to the affidavit or Respondent 2 Under Section 33(e) of the Wild Life (Protection) Act as it stood prior to its amendment in 1991 the Chief Wild Life Warden had the power to "regulate, control or prohibit, any fishing". This provision is deleted by the amendment made in Section 33 in 1991. The permits granted in the present case, however, are in lieu of traditional fishing rights of the tribals. And these permits are issued in settlement of these rights prior to the final notification under Section 35(4) notifying the area as a National Park. Hence these do not fall under Section 33.

It was held that some attempts, however, seem to have been made by the State of Madhya Pradesh to contain the damage by imposing conditions on these fishing permits. The permission which have been given are subject to the certain conditions.

Ultimately the petition is disposed of with some directions.

In this case it was held that traditional rights *v.* ecology both are important to be considered but if the right to give licence for fishing cause shrinkage to the ecology then urgent step must be taken to prevent any type of destruction or damage to the flora or fauna, with keeping in mind the perception enshrined under Art. 48A and 51 A(g) of the Indian Constitution and Sec. 26(l)(i) of Forest Act, 1927 and Sections 33, 35 (1), 19 to 26 of the Wild Life (Protection) Act. And at the same time the Court has recognised the fishing rights of the tribes as a right to livelihood of them.

Chandmari Tea Co. *v.* State of Assam[10]

Some identical petitions were also pending before the Court. As the facts and points of laws involved in these cases were common all petitions were disposed commonly by this judgement. In these Writ Petitions the petitioners have challenged various Notifications issued by the Government of Assam notifying extension of the territory of Burachapari Reserve Forest and Kaziranga National Park as per the Schedule motioned in those Notifications. Some of the petitioners have also challenged the cancellation of Grazing Permits and prayed a direction to provide for alternative pasture ground for grazing their cattle's.

In Civil Rules No. 1923/93 the petitioners have challenged the Notifications issued by the Regional Forest Officer, Bagori by which petitioners were asked not to proceed with Tea Plantation in the area in question which was handed over to the Forest Department by the Revenue Department for the purpose of movement of wild lives to take shelter in the adjacent hills during the rainy and flood season. The case of the petitioners is that the petitioner company has been running the Tea Estate for about 60 years and carrying on plantation and manufacturing of tea in the said tea estate.

Asserting its rights and interest over the said part of land, petitioner claims that for development and extension of the tea garden petitioner took a huge amount of Bank loan under the State Government scheme for tea plantation in the estate; that pursuant to the approval of the ARDC and Bank loan, petitioner company carried out the extension of tea plantation in the entire area within its jurisdiction including the area of Government land without any interference.

Petitioners grievance is that by Notification dated 13.6.85 issued by the respondent No. 6 u/s. 35 of the Wild Life (Protection) Act, 1972 the Government incorporated certain areas of Kanchanguri village measuring about 89.754 Hectors into the

Kaziranga National Park. Though as per the said Notification no portion of the garden land of the petitioner falls in the said Kanchangurin village. Petitioner-company filed objections against this Notification stating that no opportunity of hearing is given to the petitioner. Further contention is that even after publication of the notice no proceeding started to the best the land of the garden in the authorities of the Wild Life Forest Department. The Revenue Department also did not disturb the petitioner in possessing and occupying the land in question and that the petitioner was not disturbed due to the insuance of the impugned Notification. I did not approach this Court by filing writ petition.

Respondents have filed affidavit-in opposition in almost all the cases denying the allegations made by the petitioners.

It is also seen from the record that the petitioners had not preferred any claim before the collector in response to the impugned Notifications stating their claims within the stipulated time. It is also seen that the petitioners had been occupying the land in the question, some of them, of course, by paying Tauzi Bhali, revenue. It is evident from the Notifications that the petitioners were given ample opportunity to defend their cases before the Collector but they have not preferred any objection/ claim within the stipulated time and ultimately the Government in exercise of the powers conferred under the provisions of the Act, 1972 declared the area in question to be within the area of Kaziranga National Park/Burachapori Reserved Forest. It is also seen from the record that the Collector had also recommended that the Deputy Commissioner, Sonitpur District, Divisional Forest Officer, Eastern Assam Wild Life Division, Sonitpur Division, should clear all encroachers and trespassers from their respective jurisdiction before handing over the same to the Kaziranga National Park authorities.

It is an admitted position that long occupation of Government land cannot create any legal/constitutional right over the Govt. land. As stated by the petitioner they occupied the is land by paying Tauzi Bahi revenue, which is nothing but a fine on the encroachers for occupying the Govt. land. Stand of the respondents is that possession and plantation on the disputed land by the petitioners are of recent occupier and that taking advantage of the stay orders passed by this Court in 1993 they started full-fledged plantation at their own by taking over the said land.

It is to be examined whether the declaration to convert Burachapori Reserved Forest into Wild Life Sanctuary was made without having the proclamation widely circulated in the occupation area and without inviting claims and objections in compliance with the statutory provisions.

Materials on record show that immediately before the process for declaration was started the Commissioner was of appointed as Collector and all the requirements under Section 21 of the Act, was complied with. Submission of Mr. Bhuyan that declaration so made was done surreptitiously behind the back of the petitioner—Society in violation of the statutory provisions and principles of natural justice is not sustainable on the ground that materials on the record speak otherwise. Claims and objections of the interested persons/villagers were examined and orders were also passed accordingly Mr. Sarma, learned Sr. Govt. Advocate has submitted that these petitioners are not actual inhabitants of the area in question and they are recent encroachers through the unprotected border. I find sufficient merit in the submissions of the learned Govt. Advocate and prefer to take judicial notice of it as large scale influx of encroachers in such a forest land is a common phenomena, putting the forest authority in innumerable and unsolvable problems at the cost of the protection of precious endangered wild life.

From the above it is seen that the publication of the Notification and the addition of the areas to the Kaziranga National Park and Burachapori Sanctuary were necessary for protection of the wild life and also to improve environment and to safeguard the forest of the country. While adding the areas in question to the National Park/Sanctuary in question the respondent/Government followed the due process of law and I do not find any infirmity in it. It is also seen that respondents/Government invited objections/claim from the persons interested and upon such claim/objections filed by the persons fiom the area in question, after scrutiny/verification decided to compensate them in accordance with law. From the above, it can be said that the genuine claimants will get compensation on the basis of their claim/objection strictly under the provisions of the Act. Hence the respondents/Government may proceed for adding the area in question to the Kaziranga National Park/Burachapori Sanctuary if not already done, and complete the process of determination of the rights and acquisition of land or rights as contemplated by the Act as early as possible, preferably with a period of six months from today.

Hence, the Respondent (Government) may proceed for adding the area in question to the Kaziranga National Park/ Burachapori Sanctuary if not already done, and complete the process of determination of the rights and acquisition of land or rights as contemplated by the Act as early as possible, preferably within a period of 6 months. Hence, the petition was dismissed.[11]

This case was supported by M.C. Mehta *v.* Kamalnath[12] case in which it is clearly laid down that "The State as a trustee is under a legal duty to protect the nature of resources. These resources meant for public use cannot be converted into private ownership.

This being the latest case which talks about the addition of certain areas to the Kaziranga National Park and also talks about the protection of wild life and to improve the environment of the forest of the country.

In this case it is decided that declaration of the areas to the Kaziranga National Park and Burachaopri Sanctuary were necessary for protection of the Wild Life and also to improve environment and to safeguard the forest of the country while adding the areas to the National Park/Sanctuary in question. The Respondent (Government) followed the due process of law and there is no infirmity in it.[13]

Notes and References

1. Justice A.S. Anand, foreword, *Fifty Years of the Supreme Court of India: Its Grasp and Reach*, ed. S.K. Verma Kusum, (New Delhi : Oxford University Press, 2001) v-vi.
2. A.S. Anand, foreword, vii.
3. A.S. Anand, foreword, vii.
4. A.S. Anand, foreword, x.
5. AIR 1987 SC 374.
6. AIR 1993 Kerela 262.
7. Writ Petition (C) No 1509 of 1991 decided on April 8, 1993.
8. (1996) 8 SCC 599.
9. (1997) SCC 549.
10. AIR 2000 Gauhati 22.
11. (1997) SCC 388 (Para 34).
12. AIR 2000 Gauhati 13.
13. AIR 2000 Gauhati 21.

Conclusion

In the preceding chapters, I have made an attempt to examine and analyse laws pertaining to the protection of wild life *vis-a-vis* tribes. The protection of wild life is essential, but if it leads to non-protection of the Scheduled Tribes then it would be amounting to a greater loss and destruction.

Wild life conservation along with sustainable development and environmental conservation is the need of the time and it should be the responsibility of all peoples of the world to co-operate and contribute for its achievement, why alone the Scheduled Tribes ? It is high time that we must think of the Scheduled Tribes to be rights-holders, not merely stack-holders. The right of the indigenous peoples have been recognised internationally but the same are being systematically isolated in protected areas. The IUCN (International Union for Conservation of Nature) has made positive efforts in advancing the recognition of the rights of indigenous peoples. It adopted the *World Conservation Congress Resolution 1.53 on Indigenous People and Protected Areas* passed at Montreal, Canada in 1996. This policy was based on the principles of :

1. Recognition of rights of indigenous peoples with regard to their lands or territories and resources that fall within protected areas;

2. Recognition of the necessity of reaching agreements with indigenous peoples prior to the establishment of protected areas in their lands or territories; and
3. Recognition of the rights of the indigenous peoples concerned to participate effectively in the management of the protected areas established on their lands or territories, and to be consulted on the adoption of any decision that affects their rights and interests over those lands or territories.

At the request of the World Commission on Protected Areas (WCPA), IUCN's Council endorsed in 1999 "Principles and Guidelines on Indigenous Peoples and Protected Areas", in response to actions called for in Resolution WCC 1.53. In addition, several inter-governmental bodies and international agreements, as well as International conservation organizations, have adopted and promote policies that support recognition of the rights and interests of indigenous peoples in the context of biodiversity conservation and protection of the environment.

Therefore, Participants in the Cross-Cutting Theme on Communities and Equity and in Stream on Governance at the Vth World Parks Congress, in Durban, South Africa (8-17 September, 2003) stressing that the following recommendations shall be conducted in full partnership with the freely chosen representatives of indigenous peoples:

1. Recommend governments, inter-governmental organizations, NGOs, local communities and civil societies to:

   (a) Ensure that existing and future protected areas respect the rights of indigenous peoples;
   (b) Cease all involuntary resettlement and expulsions of indigenous peoples from their lands in connection with protected areas, as well as involuntary standardization of mobile indigenous peoples;
   (c) Ensure the establishment of protected areas is based on the free, prior informed consent of indigenous peoples, and of prior social, economic, cultural and

environmental impact assessment, undertaken with the full participation of indigenous peoples;

(d) Further Elaborate and apply, in coordination with indigenous peoples, the IUCN- WWF Principles and Guidelines on Indigenous and Traditional Peoples and Protected Areas (available at http://www.iucn.org/themes/wcpa/pubs/pdfs/Indig_people.pdf), as well as principles that build on IUCN Resolution WCC 1.53 and which fully respect the rights, interests, and aspirations of indigenous peoples;

(e) Recognise the value and importance of protected areas designated by indigenous peoples as a sound basis for securing and extending the protected areas network;

(f) Establish and Enforce appropriate laws and policies to protect the intellectual property of indigenous peoples with regards to their traditional knowledge, innovation systems and cultural and biological resources and penalise all biopiracy activities;

(g) Enact laws and policies that recognise and guarantee indigenous peoples' rights over their ancestral lands and waters;

(h) Establish and implement mechanisms to address any historical injustices caused through the establishment of protected areas, with special attention given to land and water tenure rights and historical/traditional rights to access natural resources and sacred sites within protected areas;

(i) Establish participatory me restitution of indigenous peoples lands, territories and resources that have been taken over by protected areas without their free, prior informed consent, and for providing prompt and fair compensation, agreed upon in a fully transparent and culturally appropriate manner;

(j) Establish a high level, independent Commission on Truth and Reconciliation on Indigenous Peoples and Protected Areas;

(k) Ensure respect for indigenous peoples' decision-making authority and Support their local, sustainable management and conservation of natural resources in protected areas, recognising the central role of traditional authorities, wherever appropriate, and institutions and representative organizations;

(l) Require protected area managers to actively support indigenous peoples' initiatives aimed at the revitalization and application, where appropriate, of traditional knowledge and practices in land, water, and resource management within protected areas;

(m) Undertake a review of biodiversity conservation laws and biodiversity conservation laws and policies that impact on indigenous peoples and ensure that all parties work in a coordinated manner to ensure effective involvement and participation of indigenous peoples;

(n) Develop and promote incentives to support indigenous peoples' self-declared and self-managed protected areas and other conservation initiatives to protect the lands, waters, territories and resources from external threats and exploitation;

(o) Ensure open and transparent processes for genuine negotiation with indigenous peoples in relation to any plans to establish or expand protected area systems, so that their lands, waters, territories and natural resources are preserved and decisions affecting them in mutually agreed terms.

(p) Integrate indigenous knowledge and education systems in interpretation of and education about natural, cultural and spiritual values of protected areas; and

(q) Ensure that protected areas are geared towards poverty alleviation and improve the living standards of the communities around and within the parks through effective and agreeable benefit sharing mechanisms.

2. Recommend IUCN and WCPA to :

   (a) Formulate and Carry out a programme of work, with the full participation of indigenous peoples, to support their initiatives and interests regarding protected areas, and to actively involve indigenous peoples' representative authorities, institutions and organizations in its development and implementation;
   (b) Provide support and funding to indigenous peoples for community conserved, co-managed and indigenous and managed protected areas;
   (c) Encourage international conservation agencies and organizations to adopt clear policies on indigenous peoples and conservation and establish mechanisms for the redress of grievances; and
   (d) Conduct an implementation review of the World Conservation Congress Resolution 1.53 Indigenous Peoples and Protected Areas and the IUCN-WWF Principles and Guidelines on Indigenous and Traditional Peoples and Protected Areas; and

3. Recommend IUCN Members to consider the establishment of an IUCN Commission on Indigenous Peoples and Protected Areas at its next World Conservation Congress.[1]

Indigenous peoples, (Scheduled tribes) there lands, water and other resources have made a sustainable contribution to the conservation of global ecosystem. A number of the world encroach and overlap with lands, territories and resources of indigenous peoples. Successful implementation of conservation programmes can only be made when it is given approval by indigenous peoples. One should not forget that it is their culture, knowledge and territories which primarily contribute to the building of a comprehensive protected area. Some kind of commonality of objective can also be visuallsed between the protected areas and the needs of the indigenous peoples to protect their land, territories and resources from external threats. Recommendation 5.24 of the World Parks Congress Recommendations (WPC) rightly talks of the principle of collaborative management attending to the needs and interests of indigenous peoples. The WPC has acknowledged that the on indigenous peoples suffered human rights abuses in connection with the protected areas in the past and in some cases continue the to suffer abuses even today.

The WWF has also been very active in this field and has been approached by many indigenous and rural communities for collaboration on issues like protected area management and the conservation of natural resources. In its publication like conservation with people and forests for life, WWF has expressed its conviction that indigenous peoples are crucial actors in conservation. Together with IUCN and UNEP, incurring for the earth, the WWF has acknowledged the needs for recognition of the aboriginal rights of the indigenous peoples to their lands and resources and they should participate effectively in decisions affecting their lands and resources.

WWF has declared certain principles, which shall govern WWF conservation activities within indigenous peoples' lands and territories. It will also govern WWF partnership within indigenous peoples' Organisation and other organisations whose activities may have their impact upon indigenous peoples. As a measure of the promotion of its conservation objectives the WWF will encourage the governments of different countries to take necessary steps to ensure effective protection of the indigenous peoples rights of ownership and possession of those lands and territories.

The WWF before its initiation in conservation activities in a particular area, will seek information about the historical claim and customary rights of the indigenous peoples of that area. Further it shall assist indigenous peoples organisation in the design, implementation, monitoring and evaluation of conservation activities. It shall also assist in strengthening such organisation and in the development of relevant human Organisation implementation, resources in the respective indigenous communities. It shall also assist indigenous peoples to legally protect their natural resource base and shall supply technical and financial support to advance even those development objectives that fall outside WWF mission. It will also oppose economic or other developmental activities, natural resources exploitation, commercially oriented academic research, resettlement of indigenous communities, creations of protected areas or imposition of restriction on subsistence resource use and colonisation within indigenous territories, if these have not received prior consent of the affected indigenous communities or would adversely impact on the environment of indigenous peoples territories or would affect their rights.

These are some of the international organisations, which have taken keen interest in the area of biodiversity conservation as well as the protection of rights of the indigenous peoples on their lands and territories and in the promotion of sustainable use of natural resources.

In India, a major policy shift took place in 1988 when the government recognised the need to involve villagers in forest protection. Accordingly the Ministry of Environment and Forest, Government of India issued instructions to all States on 1 June, 1990 that the rights of the tribal people and other villagers living in and around forests will have first charge on forests. Thereafter the government initiated the co-operation of local people through the system of Joint Forest Management.

Subsequently the government of Madhya Pradesh passed a resolution on 10 December, 1991 to obtain the co-operation of people in areas which were considered sensitive from the viewpoint of forest protection. With a view to providing peoples co-operation in whole forest areas, the State Government issued an amended resolution on 4 January, 1995.

The Government of Madhya Pradesh, accordingly, divided the forest areas of the State into three zones.

1. Forest areas included in National Parks and Sanctuaries.
2. Other dense forest areas, which are used to obtain forest products under the regular forest works.
3. Those forest areas, which have become open due to biotic pressures, and need regeneration/rehabilitation.

A number of Eco-development committees were constituted for securing co-operation of the people in all the villages situated inside the National Parks and Sanctuaries. The committees were also constituted in villages, which were outside the protected areas but situated within 5 kilometers from the boundaries of these areas. Forest protection committees, village forest committees were also constituted according to their respective boundaries. Executive committees, consisting of minimum of 11 and maximum of 21 members (except Ex-officio members) were also constituted as per the procedure laid down.

These committees along with their forest officers were assigned different functions such as marking of areas, preparation of micro plan, etc. Besides,, they were assigned a number of duties and were also given certain rights.

Despite sincere efforts from the side of International Organisations, Government of India and the Government of Madhya Pradesh these committees or to be more precise the Joint Forest Management has not been able to produce a desired result. What I could construe from my field study is that the forest officers will have to change their attitudes with regard to the villagers. The participatory approaches are not being done the way they are expected to be done by the forest department. What is required is a change in the attitude between both the upper and lower levels of forest officers and amongst the villagers.

The forest department has begun a programme of Human Resource Development for its staff down to the village level. This approach seems to sound quite convincing with respect to its goal to introduce participatory approaches in dealing with the people. The problem here is the very rigid hierarchy in the forest department of India. The officers are more bothered about the status and benefits at the village level. The beat officer or the village level officer is not prepared to share its control and power. If at all he is able to do it then his superior, the Range Officer or the D.F.O. does not want to give up his control or the benefits he receives. There are reports of non-acceptance of the ideas of forming committees from the side of villagers also. Reports of clash between different groups of villagers have also come to surface. These have to be dealt with skillfully. Attempts are being made to ensure the use of fuel efficient cooking devices in order to reduce the demand of the villagers for fuel wood. The Government of India, though, has rightly introduced devices such as *Gobar Gas* Plants, improved *Chullahs, Sigris,* Pressure Cookers to reduce the use of fuel wood, but due to paucity of space with the villagers to keep cattle, devices such as *Gobar Gas* Plant, etc. could not be successfully established. What is required here is that the State should declare notified areas for cattle grazing along with well developed modern *Goshalayas* in these villages. By modern *Goshalayah,* I mean *Goshalayas* where, besides cattle keeping, there should be relevant literature and arrangement for valuable production produced not only from the milk of the cows but also from its excreta and urine. The villagers how to prepare disinfectant, biogas and for cattle cow excreta and urine.

The new Government of Madhya Pradesh headed by Hon'ble Sushree Uma Bharti, much in agreement with the sentiments of the people of M.P., has put a complete ban on cow slaughter. It will be all the more encouraging if this Government comes out with a well defined comprehensive plan as discussed in the preceding paragraph. A State level Corporation with necessary funding should also be established for the collection and marketing of the products and its produce. I am of the confirmed opinion that such a plan will prove a milestone not only in the economic development of the poor villagers but also in the protection of forest and wild life.

Criticism for the sake of criticising is unappreciable. I would like to reserve my comments on the already implemented reforestation policies. Nevertheless, these policies of plantation are mostly profitable to the forest department. Although, the government talks of participatory approaches with the villagers, of course much under pressure from he international organizations, but if these approaches become beneficial only to the government and give hardly any profit to the local tribesmen, then its utility becomes questionable. Further, such approaches will jeopardise the ancient cultural traditions of these tribesmen. I recommend minimal usufruct rights to be granted to the local villagers living in and adjacent to the protected areas. Any policy in order to be proper, popular and perpetual should be practical and profitable. Profitability should be accountable to both the sides. The Joint Forest Management could not be an exception to it. Its policies and efforts should provide dividends both to the forest department and the local people.

Note and Reference

1. http://www.iucn.org/themes/wpca/wpc2003/english/outputs/recommendation.htm.

Selected Bibliography

Bansal, B.L., *The Law Relating to Human Rights : The Protection of Human Rights Act, 1993*, Delhi: Capital Law House, 2000.

Basu, Durga Das, *Shorter Constitution of India*, New Delhi, Prentice Hall of India Pvt., 1994.

Bedi, R.S. and A.S Bedi, *Encyclopaedia of Environmental and Pollution Laws*, New Delhi, Orient Law House, 2002.

Brazil-US International Experts meeting on Protected Forest Areas Final Report. *http://www:mma.gov.br/port/sbf/reuniao/doc/finaldoc.pdf*.

Choudhary, R.N., *Law of Forests in India*, Allahabad : Orient Publishing Co. 1999.

Desai, A.A., *Environmental Jurispnidence*, Allahabad : Modern Law House, 2002.

Draft Case Study: How the IUCN Protected Area Management Categories can Support the need and Rights of Traditional and Indigenous Peoples in Protected Areas. *http://www.cf.ac.uk/cplan/saci/cs-indigenous people.pdf*.

Fernandes, W. ed. *National Development and Tribal Deprivation*, New Delhi : Indian Social Institution, 1992.

Gopal, Rajesh and Rakesh Shukla ed. *Tiger Conservation Initiatives, Madhya Pradesh "Produce for the M.P."*, Forest Department, 2000.

Indigenous People and Conservation WWF Statement of Principles, *http://lucy.ukc.ac.uk/rainforest/indigeng.html*

Jain, M.P., *Indian Constitutional Law*, Bombay N.M. Tripathi Private Ltd., 1987.

Justice Anand, A.S., Foreword, *Fifty Years of the Supreme Court of India Its Grasp and Reach* ed S.K.Verma and Kusum, New Delhi: Oxford University Press, 2001.

Justice Ashoka A. Desai, *Environmental Jurisprudence,* Allahabad : Modern Law House, 2002.

Kapoor, S.K., *International Law and Human Rights,* Allahabad : Central, Law Agency, 2002.

Karkare, G.S., *Environmental and Pollution Laws,* Jaipur: University Book House (P) Ltd., 2001.

Khan, I.A., *Environmental Law,* Allahabad Central Law Agency, 2000.

Kothari, Ashish *et. al.,* Management of National Parks and Sanctuaries in India: A Status Report Indian Institute of Public Administration, New Delhi : Public Administration, 1989.

Kothari, Ashish, Neena Singh, and Saloni Suri, ed. *People and Protected Areas,* New Delhi: Sage Publication, 1996.

Kothari, Ashish, "Is Joint Management of Protected Areas Desirable and Possible?", ed. Ashish Kothari *et. al., People and Protected Areas,* New Delhi: Sage Publication, 1996.

Manohar, V.R., ed. *All India Reporter,* Nagpur: All India Reporter Pvt. Ltd., 1960.

———, ed. *All India Reporter,* Nagpur: All India Reporter Pvt. Ltd., 1986.

———, ed. *All India Reporter,* Nagpur: All India Reporter Pvt. Ltd., 1981.

———, ed. *All India Reporter,* Nagpur: All India Reporter Pvt. Ltd., 1983.

———, ed. *All India Reporter,* Nagpur: All India Reporter Pvt. Ltd., 1987.

———, ed. *All India Reporter,* Nagpur: All India Reporter Pvt. Ltd., 1989.

———, ed. *All India Reporter,* Nagpur: All India Reporter Pvt. Ltd., 1993.

———, ed. *All India Reporter,* Nagpur: All India Reporter Pvt. Ltd., 2000.

Narayana, P.S., *The Scheduled Castes and The Scheduled Tribes (Prevention of Attrocities* Act, 1989, and Rules, 1995 and Protection of Civil Rights Act, 1955 and Rules, 1977 Hyderabad : Gogia Law Publications, 2001.

Parks Congress : Reconciling Protected Areas and Sustainable Livelihoods, http://www.iucn.org.

Pati Jayadev, "Indian Environmental Law : Problems and Perspectives", *Central India Law Quarterly*, Vol. IX, (July-Sept. 1996).

Phadke, V.S., "Tribals in a Metropolitan Region" *Social Change*, 21.2 (June 1991).

Puranik, A.B., *Law and Land Acquisition and Compensation*, Allahabad : Orient Publishing Co., 2001.

Recommendation 24 Indigenous Peoples and Protected Areas, http://www.iucn.org/themes/wpca/wpc2003/english/outputs/ recommendation.htm.

Reddy, Prakash G., "HRD in the Tribals", *Social Change*, 21.2 (June 1991).

Saving the Tiger in Goa, (August 1999) Sanctuary Magazine from Google's Cache of *http://www.5tigers.org/goa.htm.*

Sen, P.K. "Conserving India's Tigers" *Indian Journal of Environmental Law*, Vol. I, Issue 2 (2000).

Shukla, V.N., *Constitution of India*, Lucknow—Eastern Book Company, 2001.

Singh, R., *Environmental Policy and Tribal Modernisation*, New Delhi : Anmol Publications Pvt. Ltd., 2000.

Suri, Saloni, "People's Involvement in Protected Areas Experiences from Abroad and Lessons for India", ed. New Delhi: Sage Publication, 1996.

Thakur, Kailash, *Environmental Protection Law & Policy in India*, Jaipur: University Book House (P) Ltd. 1997.

The Bhuria Committee Report, Ministry of Rural Development Government of India, January 1995.

The Constitution of India Delhi : Government of India, Legislative Department, National Language Section, 1991.

The General Clauses Act, 1897, New Delhi : Universal Law Publishing Co. Pvt. Ltd., 2002.

The Indian Easements Act, 1882, New Delhi : Universal Law Publishing Co. Pvt. Ltd., 2002.

Transfer of Property Act, 1882, New Delhi : Universal Law Publishing Co. Pvt. Ltd., 2002.

"Tribe", A New Survey of Universal Knowledge Encylopaedia Britanica, Volume 22, Inc. William Benton, Publisher Chicago, 1965.

Upadhyay, Sanjay and Ashish Kothari, National Parks and Sanctuaries in India, Allahabad Print World, 2001.

Verma, S.K. and Kusum, ed. *Fifty Years of the Supreme Court of India,* New Delhi : Oxford University Press, 2001.

Vidhyarthi, L.P. and B.K. Rai, *The Tribal Culture of India,* New Delhi : Concept Publishing Company, 1985.

Vth ICUN World Parks Congress, *http://www.iisd.ca/download/asc/sd/sdvo/89num1.txt*.

Index